T0211906

SpringerBriefs in Computer Science

SpringerBriefs present concise summaries of cutting-edge research and practical applications across a wide spectrum of fields. Featuring compact volumes of 50 to 125 pages, the series covers a range of content from professional to academic.

Typical topics might include:

- A timely report of state-of-the art analytical techniques
- A bridge between new research results, as published in journal articles, and a contextual literature review
- A snapshot of a hot or emerging topic
- An in-depth case study or clinical example
- A presentation of core concepts that students must understand in order to make independent contributions

Briefs allow authors to present their ideas and readers to absorb them with minimal time investment. Briefs will be published as part of Springer's eBook collection, with millions of users worldwide. In addition, Briefs will be available for individual print and electronic purchase. Briefs are characterized by fast, global electronic dissemination, standard publishing contracts, easy-to-use manuscript preparation and formatting guidelines, and expedited production schedules. We aim for publication 8–12 weeks after acceptance. Both solicited and unsolicited manuscripts are considered for publication in this series.

**Indexing: This series is indexed in Scopus, Ei-Compendex, and zbMATH **

Wanja Zaeske • Umut Durak

DevOps for Airborne Software

Exploring Modern Approaches

 Springer

Wanja Zaeske
Institute of Flight Systems
German Aerospace Center
Braunschweig, Germany

Umut Durak
Institute of Flight Systems
German Aerospace Center
Braunschweig, Germany

ISSN 2191-5768   ISSN 2191-5776   (electronic)
SpringerBriefs in Computer Science
ISBN 978-3-030-97578-4   ISBN 978-3-030-97579-1   (eBook)
https://doi.org/10.1007/978-3-030-97579-1

This Springer imprint is published by the registered company Springer Nature Switzerland AG
The registered company address is: Gewerbestrasse 11, 6330 Cham, Switzerland

This book is dedicated to the open-source communities. Not only did their collaborative strive for progress in software engineering allow us to compile our vision into a demonstrator—their very existence is what sparked most of our ideas in the first place! The elegance of their countless innovations deserves acknowledgement.

This book both attributes said communities for their achievements and promotes their innovation in the aviation community.

Preface

It was the 2019 SciTech Forum; we were discussing at the Software Technical Committee of the American Institute of Aeronautics and Astronautics (AIAA) with esteemed colleagues from the major industry players and influential academic and research organizations how aerospace software engineering is lacking in keeping up with the game-changing Agile practices. Legacy processes were providing low risk, on the one hand, and proven design assurance practices, on the other hand, hindering the potential for streamlined and Agile software development. How could modern approaches—such as DevOps—be adapted so that they can provide agility while supporting the regulations, such as DO-178C? These discussions led to a well-attended and well-received panel session about DevOps at the 2021 SciTech Forum.

It was then hard to find any publications about DevOps for airborne systems. There was also no real tool, technology, or solution provider for this domain. That motivated us to start research on DevOps for airborne software to explore modern Agile practices using demonstrators, to identify the unique challenges of this highly regulated domain, and to develop approaches to tackle them. Early results were published in 2020 at the Dependable DevOps Workshop within the International Conference on Computer Safety, Reliability and Security (SAFECOMP) and in 2021 at the AIAA SciTech Forum. We shared them at the abovementioned panel session. This SpringerBrief now presents the round story that reports on our exploration in using modern approaches to implement DevOps practices for avionic software. It tries to render all the steps of the DevOps cycle by promoting one or another tool or technology that may suit well for airborne systems. The highlights include Rust, the modern systems programming language, Behavior-Driven Development (BDD) using Rust, DevOps automation with Nix and Hydra, and virtualization with the embedded hypervisor XtratuM Next Generation.

We invite the reader to this first experience report about using DevOps for airborne software. We further encourage the reader to continue the development of this promising direction for advancing the current state of the art in aerospace software engineering.

Braunschweig, Germany   Wanja Zaeske
January 2022   Umut Durak

Contents

Acronyms

ABI	Application Binary Interface
API	Application Programming Interface
BDD	Behavior-Driven Development
CD	Continuous Delivery/Deployment
CI	Continuous Integration
CPS	Cyber-Physical System
FPGA	Field-Programmable Gate Array
HTTP	Hypertext Transfer Protocol
IMA	Integrated Modular Avionics
IDE	Integrated Development Environment
IMA	Integrated Modular Avionics
IO	Input/Output
IT	Information Technologies
MC/DC	Modified Condition/Decision Coverage
MCU	Microcontroller Unit
MOPS	Minimum Operational Performance Standards
OS	Operating System
PRNG	Pseudorandom Number Generator
SKE	Separation Kernel Emulator
SSH	Secure Shell
TAWS	Terrain Awareness and Warning System
TDD	Test-Driven Development
UB	Undefined Behavior
UI	User Interface
URL	Uniform Resource Locator
VCS	Version Control System
VM	Virtual Machine
XCF	XNG Configuration File
XNG	XtratuM Next Generation

Chapter 1
Introduction

The landscape of Information Technologies (IT) changed significantly in the last decade. Software used to be a product; now it is a service. Cloud is everywhere, and DevOps merges the traditionally distinct silos of development and operations. The DevOps cycle is accelerated through Agile methods. However, certain industries are still reluctant to incorporate these changes; DevOps for embedded systems is still hard [1].

1.1 Issues in Airborne Development

The cost of avionic software engineering is increasing steadily—together with its complexity. Therefore, any issue related to the software development process poses an increasing risk. To control the process and risks associated with software development, many life cycle models are available. Avionic development often follows traditional software development life cycles inspired by the Waterfall Model [2, 3]. These models suggest a rather linear process, in which the development activities (displayed in Fig. 1.1) are carried out in a linear sequence. In theory, one activity shall not be started before the previous one is finished, but in practice, this rule is seldom complied with—because the activities aren't distinct, they intersect. Further knowledge about the solution space is acquired, and many problems in the design are often only discovered during the implementation. These findings are then fed back into the previous activities, breaking the planned acyclic information flow [4].

A real effort on qualification is only mandated in the later activities. That moves all related effort such as testing and tracing far back on the timeline. This procrastination on the qualification side often results in delays, increased cost, and reverse engineering (which again increases cost). What follows in the worst case is a repetitive cycle from one failed certification audit to the next one, depicted in Fig. 1.1 [2].

© The Author(s), under exclusive license to Springer Nature Switzerland AG 2022
W. Zaeske, U. Durak, *DevOps for Airborne Software*, SpringerBriefs in Computer
Science, https://doi.org/10.1007/978-3-030-97579-1_1

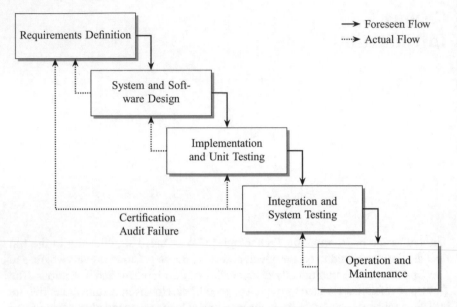

Fig. 1.1 Waterfall Model with failure feedback. While the Waterfall Model does not foresee feedback, it is still observed in the wild [4]. Adapted from [4] to incorporate findings of [2]

It almost looks like the linear Waterfall Model is bent to become a cycle, where in the worst case the initial iteration begins at the first failed certification audit. The cycle time then is approximately the planned project duration, which means the feedback cycle is very slow. When we have seen the joint efforts of the US Department of Defense and the US Air Force to adopt DevOps and Agile in order to overcome the very problems described above [3, 5], we saw only a better reason to deepen the research.

1.2   From Agile to DevOps

Agile is considered a solution for many of the shortcomings associated with the traditional life cycle models. The term was initially coined in the *Agile Manifesto* with the following four pillars:

1. **Individuals and interactions** over processes and tools
2. **Working software** over comprehensive documentation
3. **Customer collaboration** over contract negotiation
4. **Responding to change** over following a plan [6]

These pillars correspond with the difference between theory and practice when using the Waterfall Model, addressing exactly the activities where practice deviates from theory. Namely, pillar 1 promotes the interaction between those responsible for the activities, while pillar 4 portrays the need to change the development plan when there are new or changed requirements.

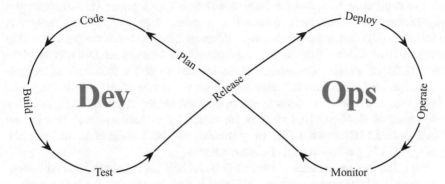

Fig. 1.2 DevOps cycle. Over the course of a project, many iterations of this cycle are desired

Recently, the Agile paradigm is complemented by yet another methodology—DevOps. Despite being widely used, it lacks a formal definition. We found multiple definitions from various, reputable sources among which were the following:

- "a way of thinking and a way of working" [7]
- "a conceptual framework for reintegrating development and operations of Information Systems" [8]
- "a collaborative and multidisciplinary organizational effort to automate continuous delivery of new software updates while guaranteeing their correctness and reliability" [9]
- "an emphasis on collaboration between software development and operations" [1]
- "use of agile principles to manage deployment environments and their configurations" [1]

While these definitions are rather diverse, there are commonalities among them: DevOps refers to certain practices, not just specific tools [1, 7, 8]. DevOps breaks the boundary between development and operations [1, 7, 9]. Automation and infrastructure-as-code are core principles in the DevOps world [1, 7, 9].

We claim that DevOps boils down to continuity with streamlined and automated processes in the software development and operations process. Not only iterative and incremental development life cycles but also inevitable software evolution during operation has been asking for rapid feedback cycles between the developer and the user. DevOps is defined as the set of practices for reducing the time between committing the code and using it in normal operation [10]. As depicted in Fig. 1.2, it connects two worlds: the development and the operation. Accordingly, it consists of two integrated cycles: one for development and the other for operation. A *Release* starts an operation cycle that is composed of *Deploy*, *Operate*, and *Monitor* steps.

Feedback from monitoring starts the next development cycle that is composed of *Plan*, *Design*, *Build*, *Test*, and *Release* steps.

In Chap. 2, we will provide detailed background in tools and approaches to achieve continuity. In particular, Behavior-Driven Development (BDD) closes the gap between all participants involved in a software project, while Continuous Integration (CI) closes the gap between developer, tester, and manager by making progress (and failure) transparent and immediate. Continuous Delivery/Deployment (CD) accelerates the release cycle so that feedback from operations can be incorporated faster into the next release—moving operations and development closer together. Once development and operations are directly connected, one may also speak of DevOps. This view is supported by various sources: Test-Driven Development (TDD) and BDD, in particular, are both claimed to increase the agility [11, 12], particularly in a DevOps context [8].

The difference in semantics between Figs. 1.1 and 1.2 is not obvious; both seem to portray similar processes, just in a different layout. However, in comparison to the Waterfall Model, DevOps promotes fast, small advances. Generally speaking, the DevOps cycle should be traversed many times during a project. Depending on the context, this can even mean multiple times a day. Comparing that to the Waterfall Model, where the plan is not to iterate at all, DevOps provides and promotes the use of feedback as soon as possible. This is an important contribution towards minimizing risk: when a feature is developed for years, only then to be recognized as undesired, resources were wasted without creating value.

Another crucial part of DevOps is monitoring. It serves both development and operation. Monitoring creates insight on how software is used and however it performs (albeit the former is complicated in the embedded domain [1]), allowing the developers to fine-tune the software to customer needs. However, on the other hand, monitored events and metrics can directly be used during operation, for example, to scale up a deployment if the usage surges. Furthermore, erroneous behavior can be detected, which when combined with automatic fault handling increases the resilience of a system [7].

1.3   Constraints in Avionic Software Engineering

In aviation, human life is inevitably at stake. It is one of the most stringent safety-critical domains. Thence, safety is the prime concern. It is central. This led to an engineering culture that is extensively regulated by guidelines and standards. Beginning in the 1970s with the emergence of computers, the use of software in aviation grew steadily, accompanied by an increasing necessity to assess its effects on safety. This is witnessed by the initial release of the standard DO-178 Software Consideration in Airborne Software and Equipment Certification [13], which provides guidelines and objectives for avionic software engineering, as early as 1981. Indeed, software became the first area to be covered by safety-related guidelines in the aviation industry [14]. The current standard framework is built around the latest version of DO-178, the DO-178C [15], which was published in 2011. It includes supplements for tool qualification (DO-330 [16]), model-based development (DO-331 [17]), object-oriented development (DO-332 [18]), and formal methods (DO-333 [19]).

The standard framework, above all DO-178C, specify the amount of rigor that is required in airborne software development for a particular assurance level using the objectives to be fulfilled. Being an embedded systems domain, many of the objectives need to be demonstrated on the embedded target platform. That hinders the setup of DevOps practices. For example, establishing the worst-case execution time or the verification of the stack usage is harder to automate than determining the coverage of a test suite for an enterprise application. Furthermore, software engineering artifacts, say it be the requirements specification, code review report, or a test plan, are of utmost importance in all regulated domains, thereby also in avionics as shreds of evidence to collect certification credit. While normally code is central to DevOps, it is now also challenged with automating the production of document-based artifacts.

It is the intersection of avionic software engineering, DevOps, and Agile where we strive to explore solutions to advance the state of the art. How can modern tools and approaches be combined to achieve DevOps in avionic software engineering? How does DevOps contribute accelerating the feedback cycle and in extent release cadence in avionics?

1.4 Structure

This book is structured as follows: Chap. 2 establishes more information on the tools, techniques, software, and standards required to implement our ideas. In particular, the development practice BDD; the relation between DevOps, CI, and CD; and both the Rust and the Nix programming language are introduced. In Chap. 3, we explain and justify our ideas towards advancing the state of the art, mapping the aforementioned tools and techniques to the DevOps Cycle while considering aspects of Do-178C. Then, in Chap. 4, we discuss our experiences gathered while implementing a demonstrator using said tools and techniques. This is followed by Chap. 5, a compilation of open points and missing pieces which are yet to be resolved. Finally, Chap. 5 briefly summarizes our findings.

References

1. L.E. Lwakatare, T. Karvonen, T. Sauvola, P. Kuvaja, H.H. Olsson, J. Bosch, M. Oivo, Towards DevOps in the embedded systems domain: why is it so hard? in *2016 49th Hawaii International Conference on System Sciences (HICSS)* (2016), pp. 5437–5446. https://doi.org/10.1109/HICSS.2016.671

2. C. Baron, V. Louis, Towards a continuous certification of safety-critical avionics software. Comput. Ind. **125**, 103382 (2021). https://doi.org/10.1016/j.compind.2020.103382

3. N. Chaillan, https://www.aftc.af.mil/News/Article-Display/Article/2171467/software-innovations-makes-f-16-more-capable/ (visited on 07/12/2021)

4. I. Sommerville, *Software Engineering*. 9th edn. (Addison-Wesley, Harlow England, 2010). ISBN: 978-0-13-703515-1

5. Air Force Life Cycle Management Center (2020). https://www.aftc.af.mil/News/Article-Display/Article/2171467/software-innovations-makes-f-16-more-capable/(visited on 07/12/2021)

6. K. Beck et al., *Manifesto for Agile Software Development* (2001). https://agilemanifesto.org/ (visited on 07/06/2021)

7. J. Davis, R. Daniels. *Effective DevOps—Building a Culture of Collaboration, Affinity and Tooling at Scale* (O'Reilly Media, Sebastopol, 2016). ISBN: 978-1-491-92642-0

8. F. Erich, C. Amrit, M. Daneva, Report: DevOps Literature Review (2014). https://doi.org/10.13140/2.1.5125.1201

9. L. Leite, C. Rocha, F. Kon, D. Milojicic, P. Meirelles, A survey of DevOps concepts and challenges. ACM Comput. Surv. **52**(6) (2019). ISSN: 0360-0300. https://doi.org/10.1145/3359981

10. L. Bass, I. Weber, L. Zhu, DevOps: A Software Architect's Perspective (Addison-Wesley Professional, Reading, 2015)

11. K. Beck, *Test-Driven Development—By Example* (Addison-Wesley Professional, Boston, 2003). ISBN: 978-0-321-14653-3

12. J.F. Smart, *BDD in Action—Behavior-Driven Development for the Whole Software Lifecycle* (Manning Publications, Birmingham, 2014). ISBN: 978-1-617-29165-4

13. RTCA, *DO-178 Software Considerations in Airborne Systems and Equipment Certification* (Standard. RTCA, 1981)

14. V. Hilderman, *The Aviation Development Ecosystem* (Aviation Press International, 2021). ISBN: 978-1-950336-16-6

15. RTCA, *DO-178C Software Considerations in Airborne Systems and Equipment Certification* (Standard. RTCA, 2011)

16. RTCA, *DO-330 Software Tool Qualification Considerations* (Standard. RTCA, 2011)

17. RTCA, *DO-331 Model-Based Development and Verification Supplement to DO-178C and DO-278A* (Standard. RTCA, 2011)

18. RTCA, *DO-332 Object-Oriented Technology and Related Techniques Supplement to DO-178C and DO-278A* (Standard. RTCA, 2011)

19. RTCA, *DO-333 Formal Methods Supplement to DO-178C and DO-278A* (Standard. RTCA, 2011)

Chapter 2
Background

2.1 Certification in Avionics: DO-178

The domain of avionic software engineering is heavily regulated. For this, DO-178 is the primary document used by aviation agencies around the globe to approach airborne software. It is recognized as an acceptable means of showing compliance with the airworthiness regulations. The document was written by a committee of engineers and aviation agency personnel; thus, it represents the consensus of the aviation community. The most recent version, published in 2012, is DO-178C [1]. Most of the information in this section is based on DO-178C itself. Therefore, we opt not to cite it repetitively throughout the following paragraphs.

Objectives form the heart of DO-178C, accompanied by the activities required to satisfy said objectives. The document discriminates the objectives required for software development depending on how an error in software relates to a system failure condition and its severity. The recognized software levels range from E to A, with A being the most stringent level as outlined in Table 2.1. While the objectives required for a certain assurance level are fixed, there is room for adaptation of activities—alternative means of achieving an objective are allowable, provided that the decision is justified. Furthermore, DO-178C requires some objectives to be satisfied with independence, meaning that the verification is conducted by a person not involved in the actual fulfillment of the objective.

In total, DO-178 names 71 objectives for level A systems. However, the lower levels require fewer objectives, with level E requiring none at all. These objectives cover all areas in the software life cycle: the development of requirements, software design, implementation, and integration but also verification, configuration management, quality assurance, and interaction with the certification authorities. Table 2.2 contains four example objectives belonging to the *Verification of Outputs of Software Requirements Process*.

Requirements are yet another key aspect in DO-178C. Not only does the document mandate requirements to be organized in a hierarchy; furthermore,

© The Author(s), under exclusive license to Springer Nature Switzerland AG 2022
W. Zaeske, U. Durak, *DevOps for Airborne Software*, SpringerBriefs in Computer
Science, https://doi.org/10.1007/978-3-030-97579-1_2

Table 2.1 Software assurance level

Level	Category	Severity of failure
A	Catastrophic	Fatalities, potential loss of aircraft
B	Hazardous	Large reduction in safety margins and/or aircraft capability, excessive workload on flight crew, and/or serious injury to passengers
C	Major	Significant reduction in safety or functional capabilities, significant increase in crew workload, or discomfort to the flight crew
D	Minor	Requiring crew action that is well within their capabilities without significant reduction in aircraft safety, as well as possible slight physical discomfort to passengers or cabin crew
E	No safety effect	No increase in crew workload and no reduction on the aircraft's functional capabilities

Table 2.2 DO-178C example objectives. Objectives which need to be satisfied are marked with ○. If an objective needs to be met with independence, ● is used. Adapted from [1]

Objective	Applicability by software level			
	A	B	C	D
High-level requirements comply with system requirements	●	●	○	○
High-level requirements are compatible with target computer	○	○		
High-level requirements are traceable to system requirements	○	○	○	○
Algorithms are accurate	●	●	○	

a strong connection between requirements, implementation, and verification is demanded. The requirements hierarchy consists of system, high-level, and low-level requirements, where most often the latter is extracted from the former. System requirements are developed from applicable standards, but also from general safety, performance, and security requirements. In order to verify requirements, DO-178C emphasizes requirements testing. As the verification needs to be demonstrated, tracing comes into play.

In this context, tracing refers to the process of connecting artifacts from all the software development activities. These include requirements from all levels, but also the code itself, tests, and test results. Starting from a system requirement, a link needs to be established to the related high-level requirements, but also from the high-level requirements to their associated low-level requirements. The low-level requirements then need to be connected to the implementation. But this is not sufficient, as DO-178C mandates bidirectional tracing. Therefore, code itself must be traceable to the respective low-level requirements. Moreover, tests need to be traceable to the requirement which they verify (and vice versa). This intricate tracing serves multiple purposes. On the one hand, it enables the analysis of requirements coverage, e.g., ensuring that all requirements are implemented in the code and verified by tests. But the bidirectional nature of the tracing allows for more: dead and unjustified code is easily detected by the fact that it lacks a connection to its requirements. Isolated test cases and freestanding low-level requirements are made obvious for the same reason. In summary, this elaborate tracing enforces cohesive artifacts, maximal test coverage, but also sound software design which is based on the requirements at hand.

While the software level is determined based on the potential risk of software failure, this does not imply that a failure rate is assigned to the software. Quite the opposite, DO-178C even claims "the likelihood that the software contains an error cannot be quantified in the same way as for random hardware failures" [1]. In order to cope with the risk of failure, among other things, partitioning (as described in Sect. 2.7.1) and safety monitoring are named. Furthermore, source code is demanded to be analyzed for accuracy and consistency. To maintain correctness and consistency in the source code, the following aspects are to be examined:

- stack and memory usage
- fixed-point arithmetic overflow
- floating-point arithmetic
- resource contention and limitations
- worst-case execution time
- exception and error handling
- use of uninitialized variables
- cache management
- unused variables
- data corruption due to task or interrupt conflicts

Last but not least, testing plays a big role in complying with DO-178C. Similar to Behavior-Driven Development (BDD), testing is demanded to be requirements-based: if a test case is not demanded by any requirement, then either the test case must be removed or the requirements must be considered incomplete. Two types of test cases are recognized, normal range and robustness. The former requires testing with plausible input data, state transitions that are possible during normal operation, and so on. Robustness is tested by using invalid input data, initializing the system in abnormal conditions, or input data specifically chosen to trigger invalid state transitions and arithmetic problems like overflows and division by zero. One could also say that robustness testing is requirements-based destructive testing, as it follows the goal of triggering defects and deviation from the nominal behavior.

Despite being only about 110 pages long, DO-178C contains a lot of information in a very condensed form. While we only mention those aspects which we figure to be most relevant for this thesis, there is much more to it. Therefore, this introduction can by no means be considered complete.

2.2 Version Control with Git

Enabling agility in revising the software is in the core of DevOps. Over the course of a project, many variants of the same file come to existence—a new version every time a file is updated. Not all changes are desirable, as some introduce regression. Hence, a mechanism to revert to an older version of a file is useful. Furthermore, when multiple people work together, organizing all different versions of the files becomes tedious and error-prone. The solution for this problem, Version Control System (VCS), is the enabler of DevOps. VCS is about managing different versions of a file, keeping track of the changes and the order in which they occurred.

Git, initially developed by Linus Torvalds for the Linux kernel development, quickly gained widespread use [2]. Nowadays, it is considered the most relevant VCS for source code, with its usage ranging from open-source communities to the industry.

The Git web page[1] promotes the book *Pro Git* [3] prominently. Not only is it presented as the official handbook regarding Git, but furthermore it provides general information on VCSs. Hence, the information in this section is based on the said book, when not cited otherwise.

In the context of VCSs, Git is considered a distributed system: developers can work with a Git repository even if they are not connected to the server hosting it [4]. To explain how this works, we need to establish some terminology:

- **Repository** refers to a Git project containing versioned files hosted on some computer. Usually, Git repositories are accessible over protocols like Hypertext Transfer Protocol (HTTP) (public) or Secure Shell (SSH) (with access control).
- **Commit** refers to a set of changes on the files of a repository. One commit always references a parent commit, on which it is based. Therefore, any commit is the tip of a chain of commits, similar to a blockchain or linked list.
- **Branch** refers to a named chain of commits. A branch is created when two different commits refer to the same parent commit. Branches are used to allow for the development to divert, for example, when two developers work on different features in the same code base. However, two branches can be merged, provided that they share some common history.

Let's presume that a repository contains an application's source code, to which a developer wants to add a new feature. First, the said developer would synchronize the current state of the repository to his development machine. Git calls this operation *checkout*. Next, the developer would create a new feature branch, based on the default branches tip (most often the latest commit on the `main` branch). As the development progresses, changes to the source code can be recorded as commits on the feature branch. Here, the distributed nature of Git comes to action: there is no need for the developer's machine to connect to the repository; all development (adding commits to a branch) can happen offline on the local copy of the feature branch.[2] Once the feature is ready, the developer can propose for it to be merged to the default branch. On most Git platforms, this is referred to as creating a *merge/pull request*, as the code from the feature branch is merged/pulled into the default branch. This process, which is also called *upstreaming*, is assisted by Git's configurable

---

[1] https://git-scm.com/.

[2] To avoid data loss if the developer's machine is harmed, it nevertheless is advisable for the developer to push his changes to the repository from time to time.

merge algorithms; when merging human interaction is only required to resolve conflicting changes, i.e., if multiple different changes on the same line exist. The process of branching, developing, and upstreaming can happen in parallel by many developers, and synchronization with the repository is only required at the beginning (to check out the current state) and at the end (to push the changes before opening a pull request).

Git is seldom used alone; most teams rely on Git platforms. These are foremost web applications offering additional functionality for Git repositories. On the one hand, some Git workflows (like merging branches, adding commits, and browsing the commit history) are available via a web User Interface (UI). On the other hand, functionality unrelated to Git is offered, for example, issue trackers and wiki-based knowledge management. All the aforementioned features are provided by both GitHub[3] and GitLab,[4] the most well-known Git platforms.

2.3   Rust, a Modern Systems Programming Language

As the choice of language can have significant effects on the development process and the resulting product, this task should not be taken lightly. Most bugs are first manifested in code, and the damage caused by them only increases the longer they remain. Therefore, we see an opportunity to cut costs and to decrease the waste of time, when a programming language is used that promotes soundness and discourages unsound code. A well-known example of such a programming language would be Ada, which was created exactly for the aforementioned purpose.

Rust is an open-source systems programming language aimed at being safe, fast, efficient, and productive. Being only about a decade old, Rust quickly gained traction, offering stable releases since 2015. But how does Rust hold up to its ambitious goals? To find out, we must look at the other contenders in the systems programming domain—C and C++. Both languages have dominated the embedded and systems programming domain for the past three decades [5]. They offer full control over the hardware combined and high execution speed without sacrificing deterministic behavior through the use of a garbage collector [5]. However, both of them bear a burden: code must be written very carefully to avoid bugs which can lead to safety and security risks. Speaking of which, it is estimated that near 70% of all security vulnerabilities discovered to originate from memory safety issues [6]. On the other hand, it is that error-prone, manual memory management that enabled C/C++ to succeed: systems programming requires fine-grained control over how data is stored in memory, while low-level, bare metal access to the hardware allows the implementation of otherwise impossible optimizations. Alternatives that promise to solve the safety-related issues like Java, Python, or JavaScript lack the

---

[3] https://github.com/.

[4] https://gitlab.com/.

low-level access and flexibility of manual memory management on the other hand. While the decision used to be either *safety* or *control*, with Rust, finally, both can be had at the same time [7]. This is achieved through a comprehensive type system, which incorporates the concept of ownership and mutability [5, 8]. Ownership of a resource determines what kind of actions can be carried out on it. The overall idea is to connect capabilities with references. A simple example would be mutability: in order to mutate a resource, the mutating context must own a mutable reference to it. The creation of references is constrained by itself: a resource's owner can create a reference to a resource only if no mutable reference exists already, and a mutable reference can only be created if there are no references at all. Of course, all access must go through a reference, so even the owner of a resource must acquire a reference to the said resource to perform any action on it.

When combined, these rules do not permit race conditions to ever appear: for a race condition to exist, multiple concurrent contexts need to mutate the same resource—which is not possible, as there never can be multiple references to the same resource with at least one of them being mutable. While this is a powerful pattern, it is very restrictive, contradicting the term *control*. For example, once one mutable reference is created for a resource, only the owner of the said reference can read from or write to the resource. To remove this restriction, Rust features lifetimes. Each reference is annotated with a lifetime which tracks how long the reference exists. Lifetimes of references must always be compatible with the underlying data, that is, a reference may never outlive the lifetime of the resource it references. In Listing 2.1, we violate this rule, resulting in a code that cannot be compiled. If the code is compiled, this would be a use-after-free error: a reference to `number` would exist longer than the resource itself. If the said reference was used then, the outcome would be Undefined Behavior (UB). In practice, the use of lifetimes eludes all use-after-free errors while removing some ownership-related restrictions [7–9].

Listing 2.1 Rust lifetime violation. The value `number` only lives through the body of `my_fn`, but is required to be compatible with any named lifetime `'a`

```
1  fn my_fn<'a>() -> &'a i32 {
2      let number: i32 = 0;
3      return &'a number;
4  }
```

Still, many restrictions remain. For example, when adhering to the rules above, no mutable resource can be shared between concurrent threads. Mutually exclusive access is however one of the building blocks for parallel code and hence cannot be ignored. To solve this, Rust allows breaking the rules in so-called `unsafe` blocks. This lifts all restrictions while allowing to jeopardize all previously guaranteed safety [5]. Contrary to their name, `unsafe` blocks are not inherently unsafe, but their safety is not guaranteed by the Rust compiler [9]. Instead, the developer implementing an `unsafe` block is responsible to ensure that no UB or otherwise undesired effect can occur [9]. This allows creating of safe wrappers for operations and primitives that cannot be expressed in code that respects all ownership- and lifetime-related rules. When carefully applied, this enables Rust to provide increased safety without strictly enforcing restrictions which render certain use cases impossible.

This sets Rust apart from many other attempts at making safe systems program- ming language such as Cyclone or Vault. These languages failed to gain wide adoption in part because they were so restrictive that they prohibited desirable instances of low-level code from being written [8], whereas in Rust restrictions are avoidable through the reliance on the comprehensive type system and the `unsafe` keyword. Finally, Rust provides a lot of information on the code. Foremost, strict guarantees (e.g., related to pointer aliasing) avoid many complications, e.g., when tracking the propagation flow of data in a program. But its type system also encodes complex information about the operations supported on a type, for example, whether its instances can be sent between or synchronously accessed from multiple threads and the annotation of data that must not be moved in memory. Together, this allows for excellent analysis capabilities on Rust [5]. This opportunity for in-depth analysis is used by clippy,[5] a static code analysis tool for Rust. Clippy already checks for over 450 lints covering soundness issues, style violations, performance optimizations, and avoidable complexity. Many of clippy's lints relate to DO-178C objectives, for example, the `logic_bug`[6] lint checks Boolean expressions for terminals that can be eliminated, contributing towards satisfying Modified Condition/Decision Coverage (MC/DC).

2.4 Test-Driven Development

In safety-critical domains, it is crucial to gain sufficient confidence in the correctness of an implementation. There are multiple ways of achieving that, e.g., formal methods which can prove properties like correctness and test suites testing the code rigorously. As formal methods are rather costly to conduct, we estimate that the vast majority of confidence is gained through tests. Hence, we figure that testing methodologies are of vital interest for avionic software developments.

In a broad sense, the objective of a test is to verify an assumption about the code. Traditionally, a developer would write some code which he thinks to be mostly correct. Then he would write some tests covering both the intended functionality and edge cases where he is still uncertain about [2]. However, there may arise a conflict: the developer's understanding of the functionality is biased towards his own solution; therefore, the test cases created are likely to be over-fitted to his

---

[5] https://github.com/rust-lang/rust-clippy.

[6] https://rust-lang.github.io/rust-clippy/master/index.html#logic_bug.

solution [10]. But there is an even larger problem: the temptation is there to continue implementing new features without writing tests for existing ones.

Test-Driven Development (TDD) solves this by reversing the order of test creation and implementation: a new feature always starts as one or multiple tests. Only once all tests are implemented, the actual implementation is started [11]. By doing this, both of the aforementioned problems are addressed: there is no question of whether to write tests after implementing a new feature, as the tests are already there since before the implementation. And by putting the emphasis on how to verify the requirements before implementing them, the chance of tests that were retrofitted to already existing implementations is reduced. K. Beck [11] describes TDD as a ratcheting mechanism on a wind used to lift a heavy load: while the ratcheting mechanisms prevent the loss of already achieved lift, TDD prevents the loss of progress in the development process. Furthermore, the test itself can be seen as a kind of specification [4]. In this context, TDD builds upon principle 2 of the Agile Manifesto.

J. F. Smart [10] nonetheless states that TDD is not without its difficulties. Developers who focus too much on details and have trouble identifying the next step are described as a major flaw in TDD [10]. Also, TDD is not very specific about how the tests need to be implemented—the level of detail desired for the tests is the subject of debate.

2.5   Automation in DevOps

Continuous Integration and Continuous Delivery/Deployment describe three practices which are often the first step towards delivering consistent, high-quality software [2]. The *continuous* indicates that these practices are about automation: some action is conducted continuously, in an automated fashion. While the three address separate issues, introducing them together makes sense: they are semantically adjacent and depend on each other. When applied correctly, these make up the spine of DevOps. But before we start explaining, one precondition must be met: as all three practices act upon changes in the codebase, the product's source code must be available in a VCS (e.g., Git) [2, 12]. This allows to automatically react to changes in the source code and is generally considered a must for robust software development at scale. As the interaction between the three might not be obvious, it is depicted as well in Fig. 2.1.

2.5.1   Continuous Integration

The goal of Continuous Integration (CI) is to have new developments merged into the main code base frequently. In an ideal world, this means multiple times a day [4]. Furthermore, it shall be ensured that all pieces making up the software are integrating well with each other, resulting in deployable software without significant defects [2]. In this context, the term *Integration* spans a wide field of objectives, which can be divided into two groups.

The first of which is building software. It refers to the process of transforming source code, artifacts, and documentation into deliverables. The code is compiled into the target architecture(s) machine language(s). While for a desktop application one would likely package the compilation products together with assets in an executable installer, in the cloud world, this could be a container image, while documentation might be consolidated in a file archive. However, only by building software, no significant confidence in its quality can be gained. This is addressed by the remaining part of CI [2, 12].

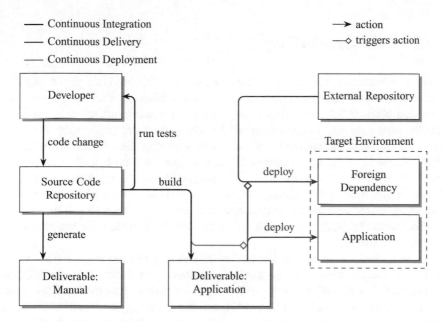

Fig. 2.1 Continuous integration/delivery/deployment. Continuous delivery extends upon CI, automating the steps required for deployment. Continuous deployment is achieved when the automatic deployment is triggered by a successful build alone

Often many approaches are combined: a comprehensive test suite tests the software's components to their specification. Code coverage analysis measures how well each line in the code is tested, quickly uncovering untested code. While static analysis detects anti-patterns, usage of deprecated Application Programming Interfaces (APIs), and dangerous constructs on the code's semantics, formatting tools detect irregular indentation and other cosmetic issues with the code's syntax. Many more measures are available, for example, enforcing that every public interface needs to be fully documented. Now to satisfy the prefix *continuous*, these steps are executed when a change is pushed to the VCS. An important aspect is the feedback loop: if the CI server observes an undesired event like a failed build/test or a decrease in test coverage, procedures are in place to notify the developers. The level of integration can range from sending emails to them to generating comments in pull requests on a Git platform, serving as automated code review [2, 4].

Just as importantly, CI also creates a common ground for everybody involved. The quality assurance process becomes visible for non-developers, and testing is conducted in the same environment for everybody. Feedback is immediate, and no human work is wasted on pointing out simple mistakes. On the other hand, making CI work is a team effort too: if every member contributes to the process, everyone benefits. We must emphasize the importance of CI: "not practicing [CI] will almost certainly guarantee something somewhere sometime will go wrong" [2].

2.5.2 Continuous Delivery

Then, continuous delivery is the logical continuation of CI [4]. Once the software is built and tested for correctness, the procedure of installing a new release can become quite complicated. To demonstrate these complications, imagine a server application that has persistent data. In order to install the said application, a compatible database software needs to be installed and set up as a prerequisite. While the required data scheme needs to be initialized in the database on a fresh install, an update might involve backing up existing data and modifying the databases scheme—followed by migrating the existing data to the new scheme. This process is also often automated on the path towards continuous delivery [12]. Furthermore, if the service is relied upon by others, it is also recommended to announce any maintenance-related downtime [2].

Overall, these steps can be summed up as ensuring that the target environment fulfills all requirements, taking care of required (data) migration, providing a solid rollback path, and managing effects on third parties. Automating these tasks mitigates many possibilities of failure [2], and that is exactly the goal of continuous delivery. Once the deployment is described in code, automation is possible, also satisfying the DevOps principle of infrastructure-as-code mentioned in Sect. 1.2. An example of a technique that implements this are the application containers—they provide a self-contained environment, similar to a Virtual Machine (VM), which is specifically made to host one application . Other than VMs, containers are leaner in resource usage, facilitating kernel name-spacing or sandboxing techniques to create an isolated environment without involving the overhead of a virtualized Operating System (OS). Figuratively spoken, containers address the problem of execution environment-related failure by shipping a virtual copy of the development machine [12].

2.5.3 Continuous Deployment

Last but not least, continuous deployment shares the acronym Continuous Delivery/Deployment (CD) with continuous delivery, often leading to confusion as both are similar [2, 4]. We think the following sentence resolves the confusion: "While continuous delivery makes sure that new changes can be deployed, continuous deployment means that they get deployed into production" [4]. While continuous delivery is the automation of the process involved in installing a new release, we speak of continuous deployment if the installation of the new release itself is automatically triggered once new code is merged into the release branch.

Of the three, continuous deployment is the hardest to achieve, in particular for constrained environments like embedded devices and avionics [2, 13]. But the challenges in continuous deployment are by far not only technical. Cultural preferences by management, staff, and customer might also hinder the adoption of it [2, 4, 12]. While some claim that continuous deployment may only be applied to web software [4], we will demonstrate in Sect. 4.4.2 that this is not entirely true.

2.6 Behavior-Driven Development

BDD is a refinement of Sect. 2.4, picking up on the idea that a test also serves as a specification. It is based on the concept of a ubiquitous language describing the system from the users' perspective. Usually, requirements go through many hands and are transformed multiple times on the way from the customer to the implementation, as depicted in Fig. 2.2: a customer tells a business analyst what he wants. The business analyst writes a specification. The said specification is processed by the implementing developers, the tester, and the technical writer responsible for documentation in parallel. The individual outcomes of the aforementioned personnel then together form the product. There is no forum in which all parties concerned refine the requirements together [10].

J. F. Smart [10] concludes that this process "provides many opportunities for misunderstandings and miscommunication" [10]. For example, when the customer makes his requirements, he is likely to assume implicit knowledge which is omnipresent in his domain. The developers, however, are unlikely to know these; therefore, the same requirement can easily result in different interpretations [14]. In contrast, BDD brings the concerned parties together, as depicted in a single step: the business analyst, developer, and tester elaborate requirements together in the form of prose text describing scenarios. This process, which is drawn in Fig. 2.2 and implements item 1 of the Agile Manifesto, is the core of BDD. The scenarios follow a parseable grammar, allowing to automatically test them against the software, provided that a parser for it is implemented. It is however important to note that BDD is not a testing tool, but an interdisciplinary team effort—the conversations are a key aspect for the clear understanding of all requirements by all parties. As the scenario-based specification is also executable, a traceable metric exists regarding compliance with requirements [10].

The dominant language for this ubiquitous, scenario-based specification is Gherkin.[7] The core element in Gherkin is a scenario. It consists of an arbitrary amount of sentences, of which each starts with one of the three words *Given*, *When*, and *Then*. These sentences describe how the software is expected to react (prefix *Then*) *When* a certain event takes place in a *Given* initial state. Scenarios are grouped into features; each feature resides in its own .feature file. A framework like Cucumber[8] is used to parse the features and run the tests [10].

Most often Cucumber is used as a parser for Gherkin while also serving as BDD framework. When pointed towards a directory with feature files written in Gherkin, it parses them, derives all scenarios, and tests them. For the testing, sentence functions are registered in Cucumber. The whole state of the application is stored

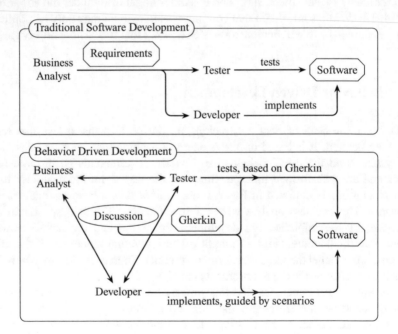

Fig. 2.2 BDD vs. traditional software development. Often, traditional software development approaches feature a rather linear flow of information, as also hinted in Fig. 1.1. In contrast, BDD focuses on the conversation about requirements. The resulting artifacts of the discussion are scenarios written in Gherkin. These are both parseable (allowing for automated acceptance testing) and human readable (allowing for effective communication about the requirements). Adapted from [10]

---

[7] https://cucumber.io/docs/gherkin/reference.

[8] https://cucumber.io/.

in a struct. Each such sentence function matches one scenario sentence (or step) and mutates the state struct according to the sentence. Matching can happen either verbatim or using regular expressions, which enables the extraction of variables from the sentence using capture groups. If a failure occurs during a step function, the step fails. Being so popular, Cucumber is available in most relevant programming languages.

2.7 Embedded Virtualization

Virtualization is an enabling technology, allowing to organize computer resources unhindered by physical rules. Nowadays, it is ubiquitous through the enterprise, experiencing increasing spread even in embedded systems such as avionics. Virtualization is about detaching the computer how it is perceived by a guest OS from the real hardware it's running on. The guest OS instead is only exposed to virtual hardware by the hypervisor, which in turn can host many guests. Therefore, with virtualization, one physical computer can host many virtual computers running multiple instances of the same OS or many different OSs at the same time. Provided that a hypervisor isolates its guests, this enables to co-host VMs from different customers on the same hardware—without putting one customer's VM at risk of being affected by another customer's VM. In an embedded context, a similar thing is made possible, running different applications of mixed criticality on the same hardware [15].

Building up on that, as all virtual hardware is defined and managed in software, virtualization allows flexible management of resources. For example, in a cluster of multiple hypervisors, a running VM can be migrated from one hypervisor to another without rebooting it. This allows for load balancing, efficient consolidation of resources, and hardware maintenance without downtime—all defined in software. Being driven by software, virtualization implements on the infrastructure-as-code principle introduced in Sect. 1.2.

2.7.1 Virtualization in Avionics

The use of virtualization in avionics is encouraged and guided by ARINC 653, a series of standards published by *Aeronautical Radio Incorporated*. Despite being written by a commercial company, the ARINC standards are internationally accepted and widely used among vendors in aviation. One of ARINC 653's primary goals is to implement Integrated Modular Avionics (IMA), which allows multiple avionic applications to run independent of each other on a standardized interface [16]. While the said interface used to be physical (specified by electrical and mechanical interfaces), now it is virtual (specified by concepts and APIs). This eases the integration while enabling higher application density, as adding new avionic applications is a matter of re-configuring the hypervisor (provided that sufficient compute and communication resources are still available). Furthermore, the effort associated with integrating avionic applications from different vendors on a shared platform is capped, as most such software is nowadays developed to target the common API described in ARINC 653 [17].

ARINC 653 employs partitions to isolate applications, as recommended by DO-178C. Similar to a VM, many partitions can run on the same hardware. In order to prevent cascading faults, partitions are strictly isolated from each other, both temporal and spatial. This means that neither one application can affect the time-related behavior of another nor can it access another partition's memory. Because side effects between applications in different partitions are limited to the explicitly granted inter-partition communication, the verification/validation and certification work may be carried out on the scope of a single partition [16]. Otherwise, certification would become very elaborate as the number of avionic applications integrated on the same platform rises. We believe that due to the substantial improvements provided by ARINC 653 and IMA, any innovation for the avionics domain must be considered in their context [1].

2.7.2   XtratuM Next Generation

Picking up on our last statement, we opted for XtratuM Next Generation (XNG) of fentISS as platform for our development. The reasoning for our choice is manifold. Together with LithOS,[9] it is compliant with ARINC 653 [18], asserting the applicability to avionics. Over the course of the past 6 months alone, the number of satellites in orbit running on XNG rose from 112 [19] to over 250 [18, 20], leading us to believe that XNG is proven in (steadily growing) use. Its implementation is written in C, and we found the code to be straightforward and simple to understand. Also, we are engaged with fentISS in multiple research projects; therefore, we are able to interact closely with fentISS on any issues.

Yet another reason is Separation Kernel Emulator (SKE)—it allows to build a XNG configuration so that it can be executed on Linux, as user land processes. This makes testing and development very convenient, as no specific hardware platform is needed. Because of that, SKE also provides substantial benefits when used in CI. Where one would have to set up a CI runner on a machine connected to an evaluation board to run integration tests in the target environment, SKE allows portraying this setup purely in software. The execution speed of SKE is very high, generally allowing to emulate the XNG configuration faster than real time.

---

[9] https://fentiss.com/products/lithos.

2.8 Nix and Hydra

Nix is a functional programming language aimed at building and deploying software—a package manager [21]. For the building of software, it acts like a meta-build system; commonly, it is combined with existing build tools like Make, CMake, Autotools, etc. For that, Nix prepares a sandboxed environment with only the specified dependencies in view and then calls the actual build system. As Nix wraps all build steps in a common tool, it unifies the UI. In this sense, it creates a well-known environment for end users, allowing them to ignore all details like dependencies or differences between build systems [22].

The core of Nix are expressions: they are code that describes how a package is built. When called, the said code generates a derivation—a file containing exact build instructions and all inputs (as in dependencies) for the package. A derivation is similar to an intermediate representation in a compiler; it stores the necessary information but not specific syntax or other artifacts unrelated to the essential task at hand. This derivation is hashed, and the resulting hash value is used to identify the result, which in turn can be acquired by realizing the derivation. This process is depicted in Fig. 2.3. All results are stored in a central cache, the Nix store. Hashing of inputs allows to robustly detect duplicate derivations: if the hash of a derivation matches that of a result available in the store, the derivation is redundant, and the existing result may be used directly. As only the derivation, but not the expression which generated the derivation, is hashed, even two equal derivations which were generated from different Nix expressions are still treated as redundant. Furthermore, as generating the derivation is cheap computationally, cache hits can be detected before anything is actually compiled, avoiding redundant realizations [21].

Fig. 2.3 From Nix expression to package

For this to work, Nix expressions must be pure: given the same inputs, a Nix expression has to generate the same output when realized. Nix has many mechanisms in place to ensure this purity: the build environment is sand-boxed and has no access to networking, user files, or implicitly provided dependencies. While it is still possible to create impure derivations (e.g., by using the current time or the build machine's specs as input), the typical packaging impurities are omitted: no dynamic content can be loaded from the internet, no previously installed software leaks into the build to satisfy a hidden dependency, and no other cache mechanism is in place to pollute the build environment [22].

Being a functional yet simple language, Nix is built only on a few syntax elements. Foremost, Nix operates on sets of attributes [21]. An example of this is presented in Listing 2.2. The `stdenv.mkDerivation` function transforms an attribute set with build instructions into a derivation. While doing so, the derivation is made to propagate a statically linked GNU C Library (`glibc.static`) in the build environment, as it is a dependency of the application to be built. Furthermore, when not specified otherwise, Make is used for both building (by calling `make`) and installing (by calling `make install`) the software. The implicit use of Make allows for very short Nix expressions on software that adheres to general conventions. The `rec` prefix on the attribute set denotes that the set's attributes can reference other attributes recursively. This is necessary as the `name` attribute is reused as value of the `src` attribute, which is defined as the result of calling the function `builtins.path`.

Listing 2.2 Minimal example of a Nix expression. The function `mkDerivation` is called with an attribute set (`{ attribute = valuel; ... }`) as argument

```
1  stdenv.mkDerivation rec {
2    name = "flauschige-uhr";
3    src = builtins.path { path = ./.; inherit name; };
4    buildInputs = with pkgs; [ glibc.static ];
5    makeFlags = [ "DESTDIR=$(out)/bin" ];
6  }
```

The expression from Listing 2.2 however requires that the attribute `glibc.static` exists in the attribute set `pkgs`, which in term must be visible in the current scope. Per convention, this is the case, and a recent checkout of the nixpkgs Git repository is present under `pkgs`. However, which exact version of the nixpkgs this might be is not determined by the expression and thus depends on the very machine which evaluates it.

Flakes are the most recent advancement of the Nix ecosystem. They are Nix expressions organized in an idiomatic way. A flake is an attribute set with at least two attributes, `inputs` and `outputs`. Furthermore, a `description` attribute can be added as well. Inputs are specified via Uniform Resource Locators (URLs), allowing for Git repositories and normal web resources accessible via HTTP. A flake can also access local files from within the folder where the `flake.nix` file resides. All resources specified in the `inputs` attribute are hashed and pinpointed in a lock file, `flake.lock`. This mitigates the dependency on the current system's state, which we've mentioned in the previous paragraph: now all inputs are purely determined by the lock file. The `outputs` attribute set may contain various outputs, including multiple packages organized by target architecture, applications, Hydra jobs, checks, and development environments. Listing 2.3 depicts how the expression from Listing 2.2 looks like as a flake [23].

Listing 2.3 Minimal example of a Nix flake. The code contains a Nix expression equivalent to Listing 2.2, allowing to build `flauschige-uhr`

```
1  {
2    inputs.nixpkgs.url = "github:NixOS/nixpkgs";
3    outputs = { self, nixpkgs }:
4    with nixpkgs.legacyPackages.x86_64-linux; {
5      packages.x86_64-linux.flauschige-uhr = stdenv.mkDerivation
            rec {
6        name = "flauschige-uhr";
7        src = builtins.path { path = ./.; inherit name; };
8        buildInputs = with pkgs; [ glibc.static ];
9        makeFlags = [ "DESTDIR=$(out)/bin" ];
10     };
11   };
12 }
```

Packages and applications are almost equal; the only difference between them is that an application must provide an executable file. To build a package from a flake, one runs `nix build .#flauschige-uhr` where . refers to the flake's URL (in this example the current working directory) and `flauschige-uhr` is the name of a package inside the said flake. Applications can be run similarly; `nix run github:nixos/nixpkgs#rustc` downloads (or compiles) the Rust compiler into the local nix store and then starts it. For both applications and packages, a default build can be specified, allowing the user to omit the application/package name (`flauschige-uhr`/`rustc`) in the command [23].

Hydra [24] is a CI tool for Nix. When pointed at a repository (or any other valid flake URL), it periodically downloads the most recent state from the said origin. Then it evaluates the Nix expressions from the `hydra` output attribute in the repository's `flake.nix` and realizes all resulting derivations into packages residing the Nix store. A list of all builds including detailed build logs can be inspected on a web UI. Hydra can manage multiple build machines of different architectures, distributing the task of realization to them. If desired, the Hydra machine can also be set up to publish its store contents in order to serve as cache for other machines.

2.9 RTLola

Monitoring is important for DevOps [12, 25] and very valuable for embedded systems too [1, 13]. However, implementing monitors is not necessarily easy. In an ideal world, one would want a monitor to be expressive, simple to re-use, but also efficient at the same time. In the context of avionics (and to a greater extent embedded systems in general), efficiency is even essential: the execution of a monitor should not impair any side effects on the monitored application [1]. Thus, the monitor's resource usage should have known upper bounds.

Lola is a stream-oriented monitor specification language aimed at runtime verification [26], presuming that the input streams are synchronized [26, 27]. In this context, stream refers to a conceptually infinite source of timestamp annotated data, like numbers and/or Booleans. A specification is evaluated on the streams, and violation of the specified nominal behavior results in triggers. Furthermore, input streams can be combined to new output streams, which then again can be referred to in other input streams or trigger conditions as depicted in Fig. 2.4. While this works well for communication interfaces like the PCI bus (on which some of the first experiments with Lola were conducted) [26], there are certain domains where this does not suffice. For example, Cyber-Physical System (CPS) often perceive the world surrounding them through various sensors. These sensors are usually not synchronized; thus, they emit their perception data at arbitrary points in time [27]. Other than that, if the feedback of the monitor is to be considered during runtime, there may arise a necessity for the monitor to be real-time capable. To address the aforementioned, an extension to Lola was developed: RTLola [27].

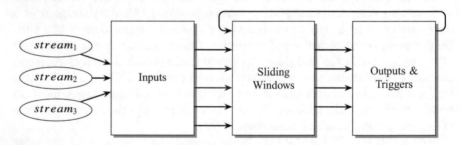

Fig. 2.4 RTLola information flow. Adapted from [27]

Two new concepts provided by RTLola are variable-rate input streams and sliding windows. The former allows the monitor's function to be maintained even in the absence of some data in the stream (e.g., when a fault prevents sensor(s) from emitting any data). As the evaluation of a trigger condition can be specified to happen on a fixed rate independent of its input signals, the monitor can even detect the anomaly in the stream. The second concept, sliding windows, allows for data to be aggregated over a fixed time period. For example, the number of navigation satellites available can be integrated over a sliding time frame spanning 200 ms from now into the past. This aggregation itself then can be declared as output stream, which in turn may be consumed by other triggers or output streams. While there are other extensions to Lola allowing for asynchronous streams as well, like TeSSLa or Striver, both lack support for sliding windows and fixed-rate outputs [27].

Being strongly typed and carefully crafted to avoid excessive memory consumption, RTLola provides strong correctness guarantees [27, 28]. Furthermore, a RTLola specification can be compiled into code for a Field-Programmable Gate Array (FPGA), allowing for a real-time capable monitor which exploits the parallelism provided by the FPGA. In this setup, RTLola is claimed to uphold the promised high expressiveness while maintaining a low effort related to system-level testing [28]. Still the research on RTLola is going on, with an increased effort on a Rust implementation of RTLola's processing engine.

References

1. RTCA, *DO-178C Software Considerations in Airborne Systems and Equipment Certification* (Standard. RTCA, 2011)
2. S. Rossel, *Continuous Integration, Delivery and Deployment* (Packt Publishing, Birmingham, 2017). ISBN: 978-1-787-28661-0
3. S. Chacon, B. Straub. *Pro Git* (Apress, New York, 2014). ISBN: 978-1-484-20076-6
4. J. Davis, R. Daniels, *Effective DevOps—Building a Culture of Collaboration, Affinity and Tooling at Scale* (O'Reilly Media, Sebastopol 2016). ISBN: 978-1-491-92642-0
5. A. Balasubramanian, M.S. Baranowski, A. Burtsev A. Panda, Z. Rakamarić, L. Ryzhyk, System programming in rust: beyond safety, in *Proceedings of the 16th Workshop on Hot Topics in Operating Systems*. HotOS '17 (Association for Computing Machinery, Whistler, 2017), pp. 156–161. ISBN: 9781450350686. https://doi.org/10.1145/3102980.3103006
6. G. Thomas (2019). https://msrc-blog.microsoft.com/2019/7/16/a-proactive-approach-to-more-secure-code/ (visited on 07/06/2021)
7. R. Jung, J.-H. Jourdan, R. Krebbers, D. Dreyer, Safe systems programming in rust: the promise and the challenge, Commun. ACM **64**(4), 144–152 (2020). https://doi.org/10.1145/3458337
8. R. Jung, J.-H. Jourdan, R. Krebbers, D. Dreyer, RustBelt: securing the foundations of the rust programming language, in *Proc. ACM Program. Lang.* 2.POPL (2017). https://doi.org/10.1145/3158154
9. S. Klabnik, C. Nichols. *The Rust Programming Language* (2021). https://doc.rust-lang.org/stable/book/ (visited on 05/26/2021)
10. J.F. Smart, *BDD in Action—Behavior-Driven Development for the Whole Software Lifecycle* (Manning Publications, Birmingham, 2014). ISBN: 978-1-617-29165-4
11. K. Beck, *Test-Driven Development—By Example* (Addison-Wesley Professional, Boston, 2003). ISBN: 978-0-321-14653-3
12. L. Leite, C. Rocha, F. Kon, D. Milojicic, P. Meirelles, A survey of DevOps concepts and challenges. ACM Comput. Surv. **52**(6) (2019). ISSN: 0360-0300. https://doi.org/10.1145/3359981
13. L.E. Lwakatare, T. Karvonen, T. Sauvola, P. Kuvaja, H.H. Olsson, J. Bosch, M. Oivo, Towards DevOps in the embedded systems domain: why is it so hard? in *2016 49th Hawaii International Conference on System Sciences (HICSS)* (2016), pp. 5437–5446. https://doi.org/10.1109/HICSS.2016.671
14. I. Sommerville, *Software Engineering*, 9th edn. (Addison-Wesley, Harlow England, 2010). ISBN: 978-0-13-703515-1
15. G. Heiser, The role of virtualization in embedded systems, in *Proceedings of the 1st Workshop on Isolation and Integration in Embedded Systems*. IIES '08 (Association for Computing Machinery, Glasgow, Scotland, 2008), pp. 11–16. ISBN: 9781605581262. https://doi.org/10.1145/1435458.1435461
16. ARINC, *Avionics Application Software Standard Interface Part Overview of Arinc 653*. Standard (Aeronautical Radio Incorporated, Bowie, 2019)
17. VxWorks. https://content.cdntwrk.com/files/aT0xMTc0MDM4JnY9MiZpc3N1ZU5hbWU9dnh3b3Jrcy02NTMtbXVsdGktY29yZS1lZGl0aW9uLXByb2R1Y3Qtb3ZlcnZpZXcmY21kPWQmc2lnPWFkPTFmMmNkYzI4OGQ5MzczOGQ1MmIzZDA1MDVmNDdlYWEy (visited on 07/13/2021)

18. FENTISS. S.L. https://www.ecrts.org/wp-content/uploads/2021/7/20210709_TheXMHypAs KITyforNewSpaceSuccessStory_final.pdf (visited on 08/22/2021)
19. FENTISS. S.L. https://fentiss.com/ (visited on 02/25/2021)
20. FENTISS. S.L. https://fentiss.com/ (visited on 07/14/2021)
21. E. Dolstra, M. de Jonge, E. Visser, Nix: a safe and policy-free system for software deployment, in *LISA '04: Eighteenth Systems Administration Conference* (2004), pp. 79–92
22. E. Dolstra, The Purely Functional Software Deployment Model. Dissertation. Universiteit Utrecht, 2006
23. NixOS Contributors. https://nixos.org/manual/nix/unstable/command-ref/new-cli/nix3-flake.html (visited on 07/19/2021)
24. E. Dolstra, E. Visser, Hydra: a declarative approach to continuous integration (2008)
25. F. Erich, C. Amrit, M. Daneva, Report: DevOps literature review (2014). https://doi.org/10.13140/2.1.5125.1201
26. B. D'Angelo, S. Sankaranarayanan, C. Sanchez, W. Robinson, B. Finkbeiner, H. Sipma, S. Mehrotra, Z. Manna, LOLA: runtime monitoring of synchronous systems, in *12th International Symposium on Temporal Representation and Reasoning (TIME'05)* (2005), pp. 166–174. https://doi.org/10.1109/TIME.2005.26
27. P. Faymonville, B. Finkbeiner, M. Schledjewski, M. Schwenger, M. Stenger, L. Tentrup, H. Torfah, StreamLAB: stream-based Monitoring of cyber-physical systems, in *Computer Aided Verification*, ed. by I. Dillig, S. Tasiran (Springer International Publishing, Cham, 2019), pp. 421–431. ISBN: 978-3-030-25540-4
28. J. Baumeister, B. Finkbeiner, S. Schirmer, M. Schwenger, C. Torens, RTLola cleared for take-off: monitoring autonomous aircraft (2020). arXiv: 2004.06488

Chapter 3
Approach

To attack the gaps in the DevOps cycle introduced in Fig. 1.2, we envision the usage of multiple tools and techniques. While a rough overview is provided by Fig. 3.1, there is more to elaborate. As DevOps was born in and for a certain domain (web-related applications and services in particular), it is tailored towards the requirements of the said domain. When adopting it for avionics, naturally some differences in the new realm need to be accounted for. Therefore, in order to maximize the impact of DevOps, we reinterpret some of its concepts and practices. In the following sections, we explain and reason about our ideas towards adopting DevOps for avionics.

It is important to mention at this point, that, despite the fact that we consider most of our work in the context of DO-178C, *proving* compatibility between DevOps, Agile, and DO-178C is not our intention. This has been done already in [1].

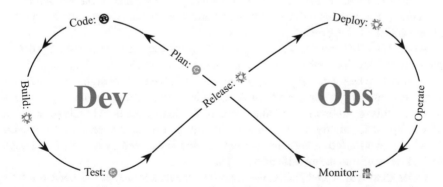

Fig. 3.1 DevOps cycle with tools. The tools we employ are Rust (⊕), Nix (✳), Cucumber (●) and RTLola (▨). All icons are courtesy of their respective right holders

3.1 Development

3.1.1 Avoiding Errors

Previously, we have identified the speed of the DevOps cycle as one of the deciding factors towards agile, future-proof development. We mostly think about ways of accelerating the cycle, but in order to reduce the time to market, not only the time required per iteration needs to be considered. Of importance as well is the total number of iterations required on the DevOps cycle, until the product is deemed ready. This number is heavily affected by the code quality and in particular the rate of newly introduced regressions versus the rate of fixed bugs.

The most efficient way to reduce the amount of errors present in a given piece of software is to reduce the amount of errors committed in the beginning, before the bug fixing. This is much more efficient than investing a lot of time fixing already committed errors. As however programming for partitions in hypervisors requires a significant amount of low-level code, it is to be expected that many errors are committed there. Hence, we figured that the programming language Rust, which promises to eliminate most low-level errors (especially those related to memory management), can contribute to ease the process.

Moreover, hardware dependencies and compatibility issues are quoted as a key challenge decelerating the DevOps cycle [2]. Rust is well equipped to overcome these challenges, as it emphasizes the use of a vendor-independent, generic Application Programming Interfaces (APIs) for low-level hardware access.[1] To give an example, this allows for the same driver of a peripheral (e.g., an inertia measurement unit attached over I2C) to be used on top of Linux, bare metal on a Cortex M Microcontroller Unit (MCU) and in a real-time Operating System (OS) running on a 64 bit RISC-V MCU. This is possible, as there are implementations of the ubiquitous, vendor-independent Rust hardware abstraction library for all the aforementioned platforms.

Also, DO-178C mandates the following: "During the software planning process, the software development environment should be chosen to reduce its potential risk to the software being developed" ([3], section 4.4.1a). Rust is designed to handle all errors reasonably, yielding correct-by-design implementations. If our expectations hold true, this together will benefit the goal of shortening the time to release without sacrificing code quality, safety, or security while serving the demand from DO-178C. It is worth noting here that the time saving is enabled by having fewer bugs to fix, not by eliminating verification steps.

Other than that, DO-178C names several aspects for which the code must be analyzed, enumerated in Sect. 2.1. Many of them are addressed by Rust: there are no exceptions in Rust; errors are modeled via the type system and thus must be handled explicitly. Arithmetic overflows generate errors, which are therefore treated

---

[1] https://github.com/rust-embedded/embedded-hal.

easily. As explained in great detail, unsafe data access (like shared mutability, use-after-free, and use of uninitialized memory) are prohibited in Rust. Unused variables create compiler warnings per default; furthermore, programmers can instruct the compiler through source code to not tolerate any unused code at all. In summary, Rust implements the majority of DO-178C's demands regarding source code analysis by itself.

3.1.2 Requirements from Plan to Verification

Requirements engineering plays a vital role in the success of a project. Having a tight connection to the requirements in each step of the development promises to limit the risk of failure. Behavior-Driven Development (BDD) presents itself as a comprehensive methodology that satisfies this: the writing of scenarios in Gherkin channels the planning of new features while forcing domain experts and developers to explore and elaborate requirements together. Through Gherkin, the resulting code is linked to acceptance tests, providing a means of verification. In a nutshell, BDD bridges planning, implementation, and testing while engaging all people involved. This is why we chose BDD as our development methodology.

However, BDD was initially thought out to enhance the development process of user-facing software, e.g., web apps. Adapting it towards other domains requires some rethinking of the process. While BDD aims to describe software from the user's perspective, only a fraction of the avionic software is directly facing a user (like aircrew or ground personnel). Therefore, we reassign the user role to the system engineers, allowing them to describe the behavior of software components from their perspective.

Avionics are often part of a complex Cyber-Physical System (CPS), resulting in challenges when applying BDD. The data in avionics is comprised of both continuous and discrete states originating from many tightly coupled sensors and adjacent hardware. An example for continuous state can be seen in Fig. 3.2, which depicts numeric envelopes that are input to multiple Minimum Operational Performance Standards (MOPS). The tight coupling prohibits the arbitrary manipulation of the internal state, complicating the stimulation of the system with BDD. Furthermore, Gherkin is based on discrete sentences triggering discrete step functions. The presence of a continuous state in avionics, therefore, requires a strategy towards providing a continuous state from the discrete Gherkin sentences. Last but not least, some of DO-367's MOPS describe change of state over time.

We started addressing these challenges in [5]. Our approach towards retrieving continuous state from Gherkin scenarios is based on a Pseudorandom Number Generator (PRNG) and a constraints engine. The PRNG generates a large body of random but reproducible inputs for the system under test. The information on constraints to the continuous state from the Gherkin sentences of each scenario is gathered. In the final step, the constraints engine mutates each datum from the random input data to comply with the scenario specification. The constrained input data is processed by the system, and the expected outcome is checked against the actual system behavior. When combining this strategy with phases where each phase is assigned a separate set of constraints, change of state over time can also be modeled.

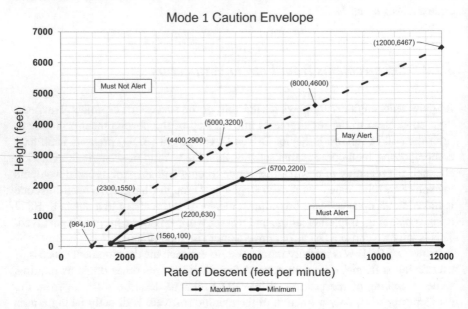

Fig. 3.2 DO-367 example requirement. This envelope is part of the DO-367's MOPS 269 and 270. Reprinted with permission from [4]. Copyrighted by RTCA, Inc.

3.1.3 Unifying Build System and Package Manager

Regardless of their kind, nearly all software products require some sort of build process. In order for a build system to be perceived as *good*, many things play a role. The build should be autonomous (requiring as few user inputs as possible) both to ensure compatibility with Continuous Integration (CI) and to spare the developer from redundant work. This plays an even bigger role if the build is slow, as then the user needs to focus the build process for the eventuality of required user input. In addition, a build process should be reproducible, to ensure that all developers get an equal result when building the same version. This implies that the build needs to be isolated from a developer's local environment. Last but not least, it should be easy to build even for an inexperienced developer—removing friction for new developers to join a project or use another team's product.

Many tools were created to address these demands. However, many of them either are specific to a certain language or are limited in their scope. For example, Makefiles are usually interwoven with the local environment (header files in the include path, installed packages, etc.), falling short on reproducibility, while Rust's cargo is exclusive to code written in Rust. Of course, there are many more build systems, but most of them are failing at least some of our demands. One notable exception is the already introduced Nix, which satisfies all these criteria. While Nix is established as development tool in use for almost two decades, we have not seen it in the avionics domain ever before. Hence, we are keen to experiment with it in this context. To make it possible, a precondition needs to be fulfilled: the toolchain used to build the product itself needs to be available packaged as Nix expression too. We elaborate more on this in Sect. 3.2.1.

Presuming that the build of an avionic software product is described as a Nix expression, that enables us to exploit Nix also as component for CI and Continuous Delivery/Deployment (CD). With Hydra, there already exists a CI server for Nix that promises straightforward integration with Nix. So comes that we experiment with Hydra too, next to Nix.

3.2 Operation

3.2.1 Operating Product and Toolchain

We observe that a vast amount of time is spent on setting up the development environment with all the tools required for avionic software engineering. When we started working with XtratuM Next Generation (XNG), this was not different, and we had similar experiences with other vendors. The procedure of acquiring and installing Codeo, the Integrated Development Environment (IDE) for SYSGO'S[2] hypervisor PikeOS, contains many manual steps. Furthermore, multiple, implicit dependencies were required for Codeo to work, but they weren't precisely named in the installation manual. This indeed is a common issue; we found implicit dependencies even in the open-source toolchain from the separation kernel L4RE.[3] To tackle the inconsistency found in the deployment process of many avionics-related development tools, we propose operations to be split in two. On the one hand, of course, the operation of the product itself must be considered. On the other hand, many tools are operated during the development of a product by the development team. This forms the other half of operations. This view is well aligned with DO-178C, which also considers operation of tools during development a concern, as reflected in the tool qualification-related DO-330 which DO-178C refers to. We estimate that eliminating any friction on the deployment and operation of the toolchain contributes significantly towards getting the product finished in time.

---

[2] https://www.sysgo.com/.

[3] https://github.com/kernkonzept/manifest/issues/7.

As foreshadowed previously in Sect. 3.1.3, here Nix comes in handy again: being developed as a meta-build tool and package manager, it perfectly suits the role of release and deployment tool for toolchains. While its reproducibility ensures that developers experience no sudden breakage in their toolchains, it also allows to unify the deployment process of said tools. Therefore, we tried to facilitate Nix to package, deploy, and execute all tools involved in the development of our demonstrator. This complements our approach outlined in Sect. 3.1.3.

Last but not least, we consider in-the-loop testing of the current development state as partial substitute for the operations part of DevOps. Without this, the DevOps cycle could not be closed until the product is operated in a production environment—which is often hard to do in avionics, as for safety-relevant applications, certification and qualification form a substantial burden towards deployment in real aircraft.

3.2.2   Monitoring the Product

We already established that monitoring is important for DevOps, but this holds also true for embedded systems [2]. When we speak about monitoring, we refer to two different things. In a DevOps context, monitoring often refers to the analysis of an application's performance geared towards refining the code. This is characterized by gathering feedback through the observation of the application's behavior, which is then used for further development. If, for example, the latency of a service is increased significantly after a new deployment, it may become evident that a performance regression was introduced. However, performance can also be measured implicitly. The share of users accessing the help function can provide insight as well—a sudden rise might indicate either technical problems or a degradation in the user experience. We've already stated that we consider running the software in the loop as operation; hence, we monitor the application in development in our test procedures to meet the specification. The line between testing and this kind of monitoring is blurred; therefore, we argue that we already address this by using BDD for our testing.

On the contrary, health monitoring is done for a system to assess its own health, to allow itself to react to failure. If a health monitor witnesses that one application yields implausible data, the hypervisor hosting the said application can be instructed to restart the application's partition. If the issues persist, further action can be taken, like altering the operation mode of the system so that it does not rely on the faulty data. Thus, health monitoring is characterized by a system monitoring itself to autonomously counteract failure. To implement this self-assessment, we exploit RTLola as a monitor.

3.2.3 Closing the Feedback Loop

There still remains a gap between insights gained through testing and the use of these in the planning and coding phase. In order to remove any friction from this feedback path, we choose GitHub Actions[4] as an additional CI tool. GitHub Actions is well integrated in our workflow as we use Git as Version Control System (VCS), on the GitHub platform. With it, elaborate details about test runs (like the change in code coverage) are directly posted as comments in pull requests. Furthermore, the platform allows coupling results from CI to the merge activity, prohibiting the merge of code which is broken into the main branch. This tight integration helps in making the feedback to developers immediate and hard to ignore.

3.3 Summary

In order to increase the release cadence for avionic software, we want to exploit BDD as a requirements engineering methodology, which also contributes towards planning and testing. To enhance the toolchain usability, we aim to utilize Nix as build system. Moreover, we use Nix to deploy the toolchain and facilitate builds and tests in CI. RTLola is intended as a health monitor in our application, while we expect Rust, which is used as our implementation language, to protect us from memory safety and Undefined Behavior (UB) issues. These tools and techniques together attack gaps all around the DevOps cycle depicted in Fig. 3.1. As BDD, Nix, and DevOps were not originally designed for the embedded domain, we also conduct some reinterpretation of the respective activities to adapt them towards avionic software engineering.

References

1. J. Marsden, A. Windisch, R. Mayo, J. Grossi, J. Villermin, L. Fabre, C. Aventini, ED-12C/DO-178C vs. agile manifesto–a solution to agile development of certifiable avionics systems, in *ERTS 2018* (2018)
2. L.E. Lwakatare, T. Karvonen, T. Sauvola, P. Kuvaja, H.H. Olsson, J. Bosch, M. Oivo, Towards DevOps in the embedded systems domain: why is it so hard? in *2016 49th Hawaii International Conference on System Sciences (HICSS)* (2016), pp. 5437–5446. https://doi.org/10.1109/HICSS.2016.671
3. RTCA, *DO-178C Software Considerations in Airborne Systems and Equipment Certification* (Standard. RTCA, 2011)

---

[4] https://github.com/features/actions.

4. RTCA, *DO-367 Minimum Operational Performance Standards (MOPS) for Terrain Awareness and Warning Systems (TAWS) Airborne Equipment* (Standard. RTCA, 2017)
5. W. Zaeske, U. Durak, C. Torens, Behavior driven development for airborne software engineering, in *AIAA Scitech 2021 Forum* (American Institute of Aeronautics and Astronautics, 2021). https://doi.org/10.2514/6.2021-1917

Chapter 4
Demonstrator and Evaluation

We've already mentioned multiple approaches towards adapting DevOps practices in the avionic software engineering in Chap. 3. To evaluate them, some hands-on experience must be gathered. Therefore, we've opted to implement a demonstrator application that incorporates as many of the aforementioned ideas as possible. The result of our effort is ske-bdd-taws-demonstrator,[1] an XtratuM Next Generation (XNG) configuration which can be executed in Separation Kernel Emulator (SKE). Its architecture, consisting of three partitions, p_tester, p_taws, and p_monitor, is depicted in Fig. 4.1. p_taws is home of an openTAWS instance, while p_tester stimulates the Terrain Awareness and Warning System (TAWS) via XNG's inter-partition communication Application Programming Interface (API) according to test cases described in Gherkin. The p_monitor partition observes temporal aspects of the TAWS partition and emits warnings if the specified constraints are violated.

We propose employing many tools and techniques which are not *yet* common in the avionics domain. Conducting a comprehensive evaluation for all the afore-mentioned ideas is not our focus; we rather try to provide impulses and show promising ways of improving the development process. Nonetheless, we will be providing some evaluation by discussing our findings gained during the work on our demonstrator.

4.1 TAWS and openTAWS

Eventually, in the 1970s, it became evident that many accidents occurred due to controlled flight into terrain. In order to counter the issue, technical solutions were sought after, resulting in the creation of the ground proximity warning system. As technology advanced, computers became capable of processing advanced terrain

---

[1] https://github.com/aeronautical-informatics/ske-bdd-taws-demonstrator.

© The Author(s), under exclusive license to Springer Nature Switzerland AG 2022
W. Zaeske, U. Durak, *DevOps for Airborne Software*, SpringerBriefs in Computer Science, https://doi.org/10.1007/978-3-030-97579-1_4

Fig. 4.1 Architecture of our demonstrator

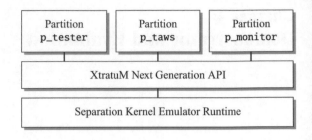

models, ultimately resulting in the introduction of TAWS by the 1990s. TAWS alerts the flight crew either if the current trajectory leads into terrain soon or if all possible future trajectories inadvertently risk a flight into terrain. Further on, guidance is provided to avoid collision with man-made obstacles and during approach for landing. One of the major advancements from the ground proximity warning system is that TAWS aims to alert and warn the crew sooner, allowing them more time to alter the trajectory accordingly. Typically, a TAWS is assigned the software level C from DO-178C. This makes it an ideal candidate for experiments regarding software engineering—it requires moderately rigor testing [1].

While some TAWS functionality, such as Forward Looking Terrain Avoidance, requires advanced algorithms and access to detailed terrain data, other functions like *Mode 1* alerts are simple to implement with little to no prerequisites. *Mode 1* alerts are triggered when the rate of descent and height above ground combination falls into certain envelopes, as depicted in Fig. 3.2. So in order to implement *Mode 1*, only a handful of numerical values need to be compared. We figure it is for this reason that many experiments on airborne software engineering are conducted on TAWS. So comes that during our research on Behavior-Driven Development (BDD) for airborne software engineering [2], we started developing a proof-of-concept TAWS demonstrator: openTAWS. It is written in Rust and serves as a test field for our experiments. While openTAWS' architecture is rather complete, only *Mode 1* from [1] is implemented fully. It is designed as a library with a lean API, in order to allow straightforward integration into any execution environment. Other than the functions to arm/disarm/inhibit/uninhibit the various functionalities of a TAWS defined in [1], only a single function to feed new attitude and position data into openTAWS is exposed.

Once this new data arrives, it is then processed by openTAWS, producing an `AlertState`. openTAWS can be compiled to freestanding targets, as it is free of Operating System (OS) calls, and currently, it does not use any heap memory. Therefore, it is perfectly suited for embedded, safety-critical environments.

4.2   Enhancing Hypervisor Partitions with Rust

Writing partitions for XNG is straightforward and familiar for those experienced in embedded development. XNG header files are included to access its API. The code for each partition is compiled and linked against the implementation of the API. The resulting binaries are combined into a hypervisor image. During that process, XML-based XNG Configuration File (XCF) files are used to express the hypervisor's configuration. Said files contain information about inter-partition communication channels, partition schedule(s), as well as resource mappings for peripherals/Input/Output (IO).

This already presents us with a challenge: we want to embed openTAWS into a XNG partition, but openTAWS is written in Rust, while XNG's API is only available as C header files. To overcome this hurdle, we implemented a wrapper: xng-rs.[2] Rust is fully compatible to the C Application Binary Interface (ABI), allowing us to utilize rust-bindgen[3] to generate Rust code from C header files. The resulting code includes function declarations, constants (including those declared using the preprocessor), but also all declared types like enums, unions, and structs. This enables one to link Rust and C binaries together in a way that both languages are able to call functions from each other.

While Rust provides strong guarantees regarding safety and correctness, these cannot be upheld when calling into C code. Therefore, all functions provided over the C ABI are marked `unsafe` in the generated Rust bindings. While it is possible to directly call into the C functions from anywhere in the Rust code, this is not considered good practice [3]. Instead, it is recommended to wrap all unsafe code in safe abstractions, providing a clean and sound API. Naturally, we do exactly that in xng-rs.

But how does one wrap unsafe code safely? This of course always depends on the code itself. To demonstrate how Rust enables the creation of a safe API, we will discuss one example in the following paragraphs. XNG's C API which we wrap for this example consists of two functions for inter-partition communication,[4] which can be inspected in Listing 4.1. According to the XNG documentation, this API requires several invariants in order to function correctly, some of which are:

1. The `samplingPortId` passed to function no. 2 must always be initialized by a successful call to function no. 1
2. The first argument of function no. 1, `samplingPortName`, is a null terminated array of `char`s
3. Function no. 2 may only be called with instances of `xSamplingPortId_t` which were initialized with `portDirection` equal to `xSourcePort`

---

[2] https://github.com/aeronautical-informatics/xng-rs.

[3] https://github.com/rust-lang/rust-bindgen.

[4] The functions were simplified slightly.

4. Beginning from the address `messageAddress`, the next `length` bytes must contain the message to be sent
5. The size passed in `maxMessageSize` to function no. 1 must always be bigger or equal to the `length` passed to function no. 2

Now, let's consider the Rust wrapper code chunk by chunk, beginning with Listing 4.2. The `port_id` attribute in `SamplingSender`'s declaration is private, making it impossible for the user to instantiate `SamplingSender` solely from its attributes. The only way to acquire a new instance of it is to invoke the `new` method provided in `SamplingSender`'s implementation. But as can be seen in Listing 4.3, the `XWriteSamplingMessage` method can only be reached by calling the `send` method on an instance of `SamplingSender`. Combined, this API design enforces invariant 1.

Listing 4.1 XNG inter-partition communication API. This is a subset of the XNG's sampling port API

```
1   typedef char *xStringPtr_t;
2   typedef uint32_t xSize_t;
3   typedef uint32_t xSamplingPortId_t;
4   typedef uint32_t xMemAddr_t;
5   typedef uint32_t xReturnCode_t;
6
7   typedef uint32_t xPortDirection_t;
8   #define xSourcePort 0U
9   #define xDestinationPort 1U
10
11  // function no. 1
12  extern xReturnCode_t XCreateSamplingPort(
13      xStringPtr_t samplingPortName,
14      xSize_t maxMessageSize,
15      xPortDirection_t portDirection,
16      xSamplingPortId_t *samplingPortId);
17
18  // function no. 2
19  extern xReturnCode_t XWriteSamplingMessage(
20      xSamplingPortId_t samplingPortId,
21      xMemAddrPtr_t messageAddress,
22      xSize_t length);
```

The Rust type `&CStr` is guaranteed to be null terminated; hence, the wrapper API does not allow any violation of invariant 2. As the wrapped API provides distinct types for producers and consumers of a sampling port, invariant 3 is enforced. The actual message is contained in a byte slice (`&[u8]`), which guarantees to be a consecutive area in memory, protected against use-after-free errors by Rust's lifetime annotations. Therefore, not only invariant 4 is enforced, but we are also guaranteed neither that `xMemAddrPtr_t` is a dangling pointer nor that `xSize_t` is too big causing us to read into unrelated memory regions.

To assert invariant 5, the `send` method (from Listing 4.3) checks the size of the byte slice to be smaller than the const generic `N`. If the size of the byte slice exceeds `N`, a specific error is returned—allowing the user to handle the situation gracefully. It's worth pointing out that this is the only invariant whose enforcement involves a runtime check. All other aforementioned invariants are checked on the type level during compile time.

The attentive reader might have spotted a couple of `// TODO` and `// fix` comments in the code. Said comments are another artifact of Rust's strive for correctness: if a variable is not mutated, one does not declare it `mut` (otherwise, the compiler will create a warning). If it's not `mut`, it may be considered `const` as far as C bindings are concerned. Considering that modifying string literals in C is Undefined Behavior (UB) ([4], section 6.4.5), the type of the argument `port_name` could and should be of type `char const *`. It is however declared as `char *`, breaking our previously established expectation. We discovered multiple occasions of similar imperfections in XNG's API by wrapping it in Rust only to find our assumptions about the code to be contradicted by compiler errors. To address them, the XNG header files will have to be changed; therefore, the remarks remain in our code until fentISS ships new header files with the required changes.

Listing 4.2 Constructor of sampling port sender

```
1  pub struct SamplingSender<const N: usize> {
2      port_id: bindings::xSamplingPortId_t,
3  }
4  impl<const N: usize> SamplingSender<N> {
5      pub fn new(port_name: &CStr) -> Result<Self, XngError> {
6          let mut port_id = MaybeUninit::uninit();
7
8          let return_code = unsafe {
9              bindings::XCreateSamplingPort(
10                 port_name.as_ptr() as *mut i8, // TODO fix to
                       non mut pointer
11                 N as u32,                      // fix to usize
12                 PortDirection::Source as u32,  // TODO fix to
                       usize
13                 1 as bindings::xTime_t,
14                 port_id.as_mut_ptr(),
15             )
16         };
17
18         XngError::from(return_code)?;
19         let port_id = unsafe { port_id.assume_init() };
20
21         Ok(Self { port_id })
22     }
23 }
```

Listing 4.3 Implementation of sampling port sender. These functions are member functions of the SamplingSender struct declared in Listing 4.2

```
1   impl<const N: usize> SamplingSender<N> {
2       pub fn send(&self, buf: &[u8]) -> Result<(), XngError> {
3           // if buf is bigger than N bytes, we can not send the
                whole buffer; abort
4           if buf.len() > N {
5               return Err(XngError::BufTooBig {
6                   buf_size: buf.len(),
7                   max_allowed: N,
8               });
9           }
10
11          let return_code = unsafe {
12              bindings::XWriteSamplingMessage(
13                  self.port_id,
14                  buf.as_ptr() as *mut c_void, // TODO fix to non
                        mut pointer
15                  buf.len() as u32,            // TODO fix to usize
16              )
17          };
18          XngError::from(return_code)
19      }
20  }
```

We argue that using a modern systems programming language like Rust has beneficial effects to the code quality. Rust indeed lives to its promise of correct-by-design. The example above demonstrates how an API can be made resilient to programming errors by enforcing its invariants at compile time and handling all runtime violations with descriptive error types. During the testing of xng-rs, we stumbled over an out-of-bounds access into a char array which however did not result in observable failure. We believe that this illustrates the danger of UB and the likelihood of small mistakes in the source code going undetected—possibly even after they caused fatal failure. The danger here is that this instance of UB did not result in a crash; instead, the program would continue executing. The existence of UB does not necessarily result in incorrect results, but the results might change for any arbitrary reason. Per definition, once UB occurred, no guarantees can be upheld—thus, subtle errors similar to this may jeopardize any other part of the code running after the UB. Every bit of safety gained by guarantees from the compiler helps to avoid this danger, and if the guarantee can be enforced at compile time, there is not even a performance penalty.

4.3 Streamlining the Requirements Engineering with BDD

For exercising a new requirements engineering approach in practice, TAWS is a well-suited use case. As mentioned earlier in Sect. 4.1, with DO-367, there is a dedicated standard providing requirements for the implementation of a TAWS. These requirements are found in the form of Minimum Operational Performance Standards (MOPS), each of which is allocated a numerical identifier. As we demonstrate in the following paragraphs, this will come in handy to satisfy the stringent tracing required by DO-178C.

In accordance with DO-178C, first the system requirements need to be selected. An example for such a requirement can be found in Fig. 3.2: it depicts an envelope used to decide whether a TAWS must alert the crew. These system requirements are then transformed into Gherkin-based high-level requirements, as, for example, shown in Listing 4.4. For this, the requirement needs to be broken up into preconditions (preceded by `Given`), mutations of state (denoted by `When`), and expected outcomes (starting with `Then`).

While this is rather straightforward to do, some details of the process worth a further discussion. Gherkin's tagging functionality may be exploited to create trace data connecting system and high-level requirements. As Gherkin does not contain a `Or` keyword, any requirement mentioning multiple independent conditions linked via *or* cannot be expressed in a single Gherkin scenario. This shortcoming is, however, easily mitigated by splitting the requirement in multiple scenarios, one for each combination of conditions. Something else demonstrated in Listing 4.4 is the use of tables and placeholders, which are useful to formulate data-driven requirements. Once high-level requirements are specified in Gherkin, the next step in the BDD cycle is implementing the tests themselves.

Listing 4.4 MOPS 269 in Gherkin. This scenario is based on the envelope in Fig. 3.2

```
1   @MOPS_269
2   Scenario Outline: Must Alert
3     Given Mode 1 is armed
4     And Mode 1 is not inhibited
5     And steep approach is not selected
6     When the rate of descent is at least <rate of descent> feet
          per minute
7     And the height above terrain is between 100 and <height> feet
8     Then a Mode 1 caution alert is emitted within 2 seconds
9
10    Examples:
11      | rate of descent | height |
12      | 1560            | 100    |
13      | 2200            | 630    |
14      | 5700            | 2200   |
```

For implementing the test cases, the code which can parse the Gherkin language must be manually written, allowing it to test the system's behavior according to the scenarios. Parsing in Cucumber is done as follows: a data type is defined, which contains the state of the application. The said type is assigned a default value, resulting in a reproducible initial state. For each sentence type (Given, When, and Then), a function can be registered, which matches against the sentence using a string or regular expression. If the former mechanism is used, Cucumber simply checks whether the sentence matches the string. If it does, the function is executed with a mutable reference to the application state type, allowing it to modify or examine the application's state according to the sentence. When looking at Listing 4.4, this would result in many almost identical sentences, for example, three sentences for the three rate of descent values found in the table. To avoid this, regular expressions can be exploited: the function implementing a sentence is registered with a regular expression, allowing to match Chomsky Type-3 grammars in each sentence. Through capture groups (denoted by parenthesis), elements can be extracted from the sentence. Listing 4.5 demonstrates how this comes into play: two capture groups are used to extract both the type of condition (at most or at least) and the numerical limit defined in the sentence. The first argument (world) is the mutable reference to the struct containing all application state mentioned above.

Listing 4.5 Parser function in Cucumber. This function can parse the first When sentence from the Gherkin scenario in Listing 4.4

```
1   #[when(regex = r"^the rate of descent is at (most|least) (\d+)
        feet per minute$")]
2   fn rate_of_descent(world: &mut MyWorld, most_or_least: String,
        rod: f64) {
3       let rod = Velocity::new::<foot_per_minute>(rod);
4       match most_or_least.as_str() {
5           "most" => {
6               // ...
7           }
8           "least" => {
9               // ...
10          }
11          _ => {
12              panic!("unable to parse this sentence");
13          }
14      }
15  }
```

To demonstrate the capabilities of this regular expression-based matching, we've compiled a list of concrete sentences which are all parseable by the function from Listing 4.5. To clarify the capture groups' functionality, all extracted information is underlined.

- When the rate of descent is at least 5700 feet per minute
- When the rate of descent is at least 1798 feet per minute
- When the rate of descent is at most 964 feet per minute

Upon closer inspection of Listing 4.5, one may ask how the regular expression (preceded by `regex =`) is connected to the function `rate_of_descent`. Rust allows for macros to read and modify code. During compilation, a macro named `when` is called with the argument `regex` on the function `rate_of_descent`. First, the said macro analyzes the regular expression and determines that it contains two capture groups. All but the first argument to the function are then mapped to the capture groups; the macro expects the function on which it is called to have exactly one argument more than there are capture groups in its regular expression. As the macro knows not only the name but also the type of the function's arguments, it also tries to select a proper way of converting the string extracted by a capture group to the target type, e.g., the `rod` argument is parsed into a `f64`. Finally, the required code is generated to register this step function with the Cucumber framework. Macro-based code expansion allows for a very concise and powerful parser implementation in the Cucumber framework.

We hinted in Sect. 3.1.2 that some adaptation is necessary for BDD to work well with the kind of data-driven requirements often found in the avionics domain. Therefore, we've developed the press-mold strategy:

Instead of directly stimulating the system, each Gherkin sentence which describes a constraint on the input data is transformed into a press-mold function. When called, the said function receives input data which then is transformed into the specified numeric range(s). A pseudorandom number generator is used to generate a lot of reproducible yet evenly distributed input data, for example, 10,000 random aircraft states. Now to test a scenario, each of its sentences is parsed. Sentences describing a simple state change on the TAWS, for example, "Given Mode 1 is inhibited," are directly carried out on the TAWS. If however a sentence describes a constraint on input data (e.g., "When the height above terrain is between 100 and 2200 feet"), a press-mold function is generated. For each scenario, all such functions are collected. In the final stage of the scenario, the `Then` sentence, the random input data is transformed through the press-mold functions. After each press-mold function was applied, the input data complies with all constraints described in the previous sentences of the scenario. The transformed data then is fed to the TAWS, and its reaction is compared with the expected outcome described in the `Then` sentence.

To comply with the partitioned environment, Cucumber and openTAWS reside in separate partitions (as shown in Fig. 4.1). All communication between them is conducted over sampling ports provided by the XNG API. This allows to maintain a realistic test environment: from the perspective of the `p_taws` partition, there is no difference between testing with cucumber and running in production. This is important for avionics or as DO-178C states it: "A preferred test environment includes the software [...] tested in an environment that closely resembles the behavior of the target computer environment."

Also, it satisfies many of the traceability requirements mandated by DO-178C. The tagging of high-level requirements in Gherkin with their respective MOPS establishes a bidirectional link between system and high-level requirements. As requirements written in Gherkin are also test cases, naturally tests are also traceable to requirements (and vice versa). The result of running all tests in Cucumber provides detailed insight on the current coverage of requirements, which in BDD is even called automated acceptance testing [5]. Finally, code coverage tools can be used to generate trace data connecting implementation with requirements, by observing which code is executed by all test cases associated with a requirement.

BDD emphasizes the work on requirements and verification before any code is written, keeping the requirements always in mind during the implementation. This both fulfills the requirements-driven process mandated by DO-178C and enables project managers and stakeholders to have a detailed insight on the project's current status and recent progress. J. F. Smart [5] argues that this helps to address both of the big risks in software development: not building the software right and not building the right software [5]. Contrary to this sections title, BDD does not only streamline the requirements engineering—it benefits the whole development process. The reason for this is simple: requirements play an important role from beginning to end of a project; hence, any improvement related to requirements is beneficial to the whole project as well.

4.4   Continuous Integration

4.4.1   GitHub Actions

As already disclosed, openTAWS development takes place on GitHub, a popular Git platform. Recently, GitHub launched their own Continuous Integration (CI) service, GitHub Actions,[5] which we were keen to try. The promise is that GitHub Actions is well integrated in the overall GitHub platform, allowing for a seamless experience. At its core, GitHub Actions interprets workflow files. A workflow consists of jobs, of which each may contain multiple steps. These steps (or actions) range from fetching source code to building a deliverable or running a test suite. Actions can be wrapped up as reusable, configurable modules, with a marketplace to browse available modules. In order to explore the extent of CI used for ske-bdd-taws-demonstrator, we will discuss the jobs in the respective workflow file one by one.

The first two jobs are about static code analysis. Each partition's code is analyzed for incorrect indentation—if any is found, a new commit fixing the indentation is added. Further on, the static analysis tool clippy is used to spot issues and anti-patterns in the code. For instance, if the length of a vector is checked to be zero (`my_vec.len() == 0`), clippy will point out that there is a dedicated function for that operation (`my_vec.is_empty()`). It is furthermore possible to instruct the Rust compiler (and clippy) to enforce various quality aspects on the code. The compiler, for example, can be configured to treat the use of `unsafe` code or the existence of public API without documentation as an error, terminating the compilation. The

---

[5] https://github.com/features/actions.

level of warnings and errors can be configured down to a single line of code, enabling for fine-grained exceptions from conventions. This allows configuring a rather strict set of code conventions without an inescapable compulsion for some compiler warnings to be accepted. The metric of acceptance can thus be very simple: the code is fine if it yields no warnings and no errors.

The next job is building the XNG configuration. This is preceded by fetching SKE from another private repository, as the partitions have to link against SKE's object code. The build consists of two stages. In stage 1, all partitions are compiled to object code. In stage 2, the partitions' object code is linked together with the required libraries, such as the SKE runtime. This results in partition images, which can be loaded in SKE. Last, the fully compiled XNG configuration consisting of partition images, configuration in the form of XCF, Gherkin features, and RTLola specification are stored as build artifact to allow retrieval in the subsequent jobs.

We built a small wrapper for SKE in Rust, ske-rs, which became our tool of choice to invoke the SKE runtime. With ske-rs however, we hit a significant shortcoming of GitHub Actions. It is currently not possible to share build artifacts between multiple repositories. Therefore, since ske-rs' source code resides in its own repository, we had to insert yet another job in the ske-bdd-taws-demonstrator workflow solely to compile ske-rs.

Once both the XNG configuration and ske-rs are built, the final job is testing. It executes the XNG configuration in SKE while collecting all messages emitted. These messages provide evidence regarding any violation of the requirements. All information gathered by the jobs is accessible in GitHub's web User Interface (UI). Whenever a pull request for the default branch is opened, all jobs are executed. This ensures that code quality issues are directly brought to the developers' attention. To lower the friction involved in the process even further, our GitHub Actions workflow is configured to cache most immediate results—resulting in even less delay from code change to feedback.

The seamless integration between source code, issue tracker, pull requests, and CI/Continuous Delivery/Deployment (CD) make a compelling argument for GitHub Actions and similar platforms. Based on our experience this far, we can only recommend trying the GitHub Actions ecosystem for developments on GitHub. However, we identified a few issues with it too. As previously mentioned, GitHub Actions does not provide a native channel to share artifacts between different workflows. Considering the somewhat complicated dependency graph depicted in Fig. 4.2, this caused us to rebuild dependencies in the workflows of their downstream consumers. This problem becomes bigger with every additional repository involved and hence hinders the upscaling of development. Also while not a strict requirement, we fancy having as few differences in between the development environment on a developer's machine and the CI/CD environment as possible. Last but not least, the platform as a service model offered by GitHub might be incompatible with the requirements of confidential and commercial projects. This together led us to another approach: Nix.

4.4.2   Nix and Hydra

In Fig. 3.1, we promised Nix to contribute in the activities of building, releasing, and deploying software. To understand how Nix enhances these, first we must establish the actors involved. SKE is required both to compile our XNG configuration and to run it. Each partition introduced in Fig. 4.1 is a Rust package, and all three together form a workspace. All partitions also depend on xng-rs, our Rust API wrapper. And, while not directly subject of this thesis, openTAWS is a central dependency used by p_taws. The relations between all these repositories are outlined in Fig. 4.2. But how does Nix contribute here? To answer this question, we focus on the user experience of using Nix in our project.

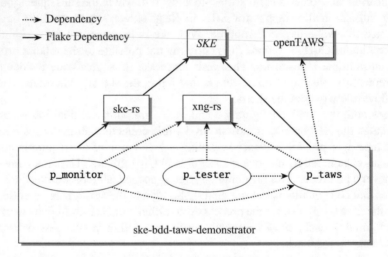

Fig. 4.2 Dependency graph of our demonstrator. Each rectangle is a repository, ellipses represent partitions, and private repositories are in *italic*

Foremost, we implemented Nix flakes for all the repositories depicted. This allows for a remarkably streamlined UI; acquiring and executing a copy of ske-rs boils down to running `nix run github:aeronautical-informatics/ske-rs` in a shell. Building the main branch of ske-bdd-taws-demonstrator is as straightforward; running `nix build github:aeronautical-informatics/ske-bdd-taws-demonstrator` suffices. The integration with Hydra is conducted in a similar pace: the flake Uniform Resource Locator (URL) and a handful of metadata (like the poll rate in seconds) are configured. Once it is ensured that the Hydra user can access the flake's URL, for example, by adding the Hydra user's Secure Shell (SSH) key to the repositories access list, CI is set up.

It is worth pointing out that since SKE is a commercial product, we are not able to make it publicly available. To cope with the limitation, our copy of SKE resides in a private Git repository. All developers of our team are granted access to that repository, via SSH-based authentication. The same holds true for our Hydra machine; its user's SSH key is too registered as allowed user in the SKE repository.

Unfortunately, being able to build a package with a single command is not always sufficient. Often it is desirable to tinker with the build environment, for example, to inspect intermediate build artifacts, or to try different compiler flags. The `outputs.devShell` attribute in a flake is used to provide a shell environment with all build tools available. This allows to run only some build steps followed by an examination of the results. Through this, continuous delivery of development environments is achieved: deploying followed by using a development environment is as simple as running `nix develop` in the project directory. With NixOS,[6] there is even a Linux distribution based on Nix. When running NixOS, the full development machine's configuration can be managed (and continuously deployed) using Nix, paving the way towards a full infrastructure-as-code setup. This is why we argue that continuous deployment is feasible for more than web applications.

Nix solves most issues we encountered with GitHub Actions. The Nix store serves as universal build cache, avoiding any unnecessary rebuilds. As the cache can be shared via network, this holds true even between CI server and developer machine. Furthermore, with Hydra, the differences between CI and local build environment can be eliminated—both realize the same derivations. Since one is free to self-host all involved infrastructure, any dependence on other service vendors is avoided. When put together, this demonstrates a compelling use case for Nix. However, this solution does not even come close to being as tightly integrated with the development as CI services provided by Git platforms are. The use of Hydra is not prescriptive; Nix can be used equally well inside of CI services like GitHub Actions. It depends on a specific project's demands how much Nix should be used. Fortunately, no risk is associated with trying Nix; one only has to add a `flake.nix` and a `flake.lock` file to the repository.

4.5 Monitoring with RTLola

We propose RTLola as a monitoring tool in Fig. 3.1. First let's recall what monitoring is about: some data surveyed on a system is monitored for abnormal behavior, in order to detect failure. As avionics often is related to safety, this forms yet another concern for a monitor. DO-178C defines a safety monitor as follows: "A means of

---

[6] https://nixos.org/.

protecting against specific failure conditions by directly monitoring a function for failures that would result in a failure condition" [6]. Now, to implement a (safety) monitor, some preconditions must be fulfilled. One needs to know what behavior of the system is considered nominal, in order to decide whether a certain behavior deviates from the norm. This knowledge must be transformed in an executable representation. For the monitor to witness anything, the data to be observed must also be accessible to it. Last, if a safety monitor is sought after, a mechanism is required to react to a witnessed failure. The monitoring framework of our choice—RTLola—offers broad functionality towards observing temporal aspects. We opt to implement temporal runtime monitors in it and also exercise how to complement the existing Cucumber test suite.

When reconsidering Listing 4.4, the Then sentence stands out for its suffix "within 2 seconds." This is due to DO-367 mandating TAWS to no exceed a maximal delay between arrival of a situation justifying alert and the actual alert. We've decided for the TAWS to operate at 2 Hz, which satisfies the aforementioned temporal requirements mandated by DO-367. A failure of TAWS could be due to multiple reasons. Either the TAWS fails to emit new alert states, or there is a lack of new input data for the TAWS. To allow for fine-grained fault detection of both mentioned scenarios, we broke down the requirement further: not only has the p_taws partition to emit new alerts with 2 Hz, but new input data (aircraft state) needs to arrive at least at the same rate too. We arbitrarily mandate input data to be updated on an even higher frequency of 25 Hz. Now that two requirements were identified, the next question is: how to implement a monitor for them?

To answer this question, we discuss the RTLola specification provided in Listing 4.6. RTLola is based on streams of input data—in this case, two inputs are defined, containing the timestamps for when a new aircraft/alert state is propagated to the monitor. An output stream is generated at 25 Hz based on the arrival of new aircraft state: check_aircraft_state_rate. It uses a sliding time window to count the number of new state arrivals over the last second. As we required the input data to be available at 25 Hz, any number lower than 25 indicates a failure. Now to measure p_taws latency, the difference in time between arrival of new aircraft state and new alert state is to be considered. This time is calculated whenever a new alert state (output from the TAWS) arrives. The result of the said calculation is assigned to the output stream check_taws_alert_delay. Trigger conditions based on this output stream reveal information about the systems health: either the "TAWS is responsive" or it violated the mandated 500 ms update interval.

Listing 4.6 Example RTLola specification

```
1  // timestamp of new aircraft state
2  input new_aircraft_state: Float64
3
4  // timestamp of a new alert state
5  input new_alert_state: Float64
6
7  output check_aircraft_state_rate @ 25Hz :=
       new_aircraft_state.aggregate(over_exactly: 1s, using:
       count).defaults(to: 0) < 25
8  output check_taws_alert_delay @ new_alert_state :=
       new_alert_state - new_aircraft_state.hold(or: 0.0)
9
10 trigger check_aircraft_state_rate "Receival of new aircraft
       states infrequent"
11 trigger check_taws_alert_delay >= 0.5 "TAWS did not emit alert
       state within 0.5 seconds after aircraft state"
12 trigger check_taws_alert_delay < 0.5 "TAWS is responsive"
```

Once the RTLola specification itself is ready, the next step consists of integrating the monitor into our XNG configuration. Figure 4.1 already depicts a partition for the monitor. Nevertheless, to allow the monitor to function, a time slot must also be allocated after each partition it monitors. Furthermore, the data under observation itself must be available too. The former is achieved by altering the schedule accordingly—we added a 10 ms slot for p_monitor after every other partition in the schedule. To allow the latter, we modified the inter-partition channel mapping in a way, so that every message is also sent to p_monitor. This is one way of allowing it to capture timestamps corresponding to the arrival of new data from p_tester and p_taws.

Integrating RTLola was fairly straightforward, which speaks for it. The most complicated part of building a safety monitor is to ensure that it is capable of real-time execution while maintaining known upper bounds regarding the memory consumption. This burden is taken away by RTLola, as the specification language that is designed to support this very use case. Withal, RTLola could use some more polishing—there are ergonomic issues in its API, and the documentation is rather sparse. We expect this to improve significantly as the Rust implementation of RTLola matures; hence, we do not consider these flaws to be principal reasons against using RTLola in the future.

References

1. RTCA, *DO-367 Minimum Operational Performance Standards (MOPS) for Terrain Awareness and Warning Systems (TAWS) Airborne Equipment* (Standard. RTCA, 2017)
2. W. Zaeske, U. Durak, C. Torens, Behavior driven development for airborne software engineering, in *AIAA Scitech 2021 Forum* (American Institute of Aeronautics and Astronautics, 2021). https://doi.org/10.2514/6.2021-1917

3. S. Klabnik, C. Nichols, *The Rust Programming Language* (2021). https://doc.rust-lang.org/stable/book/ (visited on 05/26/2021)
4. ISO, *Information technology—Programming languages—C* Standard (International Organization for Standardization, Geneva, 2017)
5. J.F. Smart, *BDD in Action Behavior-Driven Development for the Whole Software Lifecycle* (Manning Publications, Birmingham, 2014). ISBN: 978-1-617-29165-4
6. RTCA, *DO-178C Software Considerations in Airborne Systems and Equipment Certification.* Standard (RTCA, 2011)

Chapter 5
Outlook and Conclusion

5.1 Outlook

As this text promotes many ideas incorporating various tools, of course, there are a lot of open points. Some things do not satisfy all relevant desires yet, others plainly do not work, and much more can be said and done than what has been mentioned so far. In the following sections, we highlight some of these points in order to guide the future discussions and admit the shortcomings in our work.

5.1.1 Modify Setup for Full XNG Compatibility

The current ske-bdd-taws-demonstrator setup depends on a Linux environment for both the `p_tester` and the `p_monitor` partition. While this works in Separation Kernel Emulator (SKE), it does not in XtratuM Next Generation (XNG). For `p_tester`, we foresee the usage of an embedded Linux running as partition to provide the required runtime environment. This partition then can be used not only to run a Cucumber test-suite but also for manual debugging as interactive inspection of the running system is possible. XNG is already well equipped to allow for this, as fentISS offers a Linux fork specifically designed to run in a partition.

For the RTLola-based `p_monitor` partition, we hope to eventually drop this constraint once RTLola can be compiled to freestanding targets. Unfortunately, our distribution of SKE does not implement most of XNG's health monitoring services, hindering the integration of RTLola significantly. Our ideas towards improving these are outlined in Sect. 5.1.3.

© The Author(s), under exclusive license to Springer Nature Switzerland AG 2022
W. Zaeske, U. Durak, *DevOps for Airborne Software*, SpringerBriefs in Computer
Science, https://doi.org/10.1007/978-3-030-97579-1_5

5.1.2 Allow for Code Coverage Analysis

As of writing, SKE is only available for the x86 architecture. However, our development is geared towards ARM platforms. Hence, we cannot run the same object code in SKE as on the target platform. Depending on the software level, DO-178C mandates code coverage analysis on the target machine's object code, which thus cannot be achieved with the current setup. This is unfortunate, as we believe software-based object code coverage analysis to be a real enhancement in a DevOps toolchain. We envision the usage of some emulator like QEMU[1] for software tracing in order to gather the required coverage data. The feasibility of this approach is yet to be determined.

5.1.3 RTLola and Rust for Resilience

Once RTLola matures enough, we are eager to build a resilience framework on top of it. We imagine a declarative approach which provides resilience even for legacy systems. In it, RTLola is used to declare events relevant to the system's health (both positive indicators and fault events), while a reaction library provides means of countering errors. A declarative rule-work specified by the system integrator then wires events to reaction library, allowing the system to prevent failure. This process doesn't need to be fully autonomous, e.g., if multiple reactions seem to be well suited for a situation, humans may be consulted to choose an action from a preselection. This would not only implement what DO-178C defines as a safety monitor but also could be combined with adaptive runtime reconfiguration.

5.1.4 Online Monitoring for Software Planning

For this text, we focused on safety monitoring, meaning the gathering of information on the system with the intent to use the said information on the same system. However, in the DevOps context, monitoring means a lot more: it is meant to provide new inputs towards the software planning, not only to mitigate failure at runtime. Once avionics become even more connected, a scenario where live data is sent back to the vendor becomes feasible. This would enable powerful development practices, as detailed insight in the usage and utilization of applications and platforms becomes available. We hope that this kind of monitoring will eventually see widespread use in the industry.

---

[1] https://www.qemu.org/.

5.1.5   Operating Development Grade Products in Real Aircraft

Picking up on the previous section, other DevOps practices like A/B testing might also be adapted for airborne software engineering. In A/B testing, a new version of an application is deployed only partial, in order to compare its behavior with the current production system. For this thesis, we did however presume that the operation is limited to in-the-loop testing. Further research towards operating development builds of avionic software in real aircraft seems promising. We envision a scenario where the development build is ran side by side to the traditional three-lane setup. A fourth lane hosts the development build, which is only connected to inputs but not to actuators. The outputs of the development build are continuously monitored and can later be compared with the outputs of the three lanes in active use. This mechanism allows to gather great insight into the functionality (and possible regressions) of the development build without any reduction in operational safety of the aircraft in use. The input data would be of exceptional plausibility, being capture on a real system.

5.1.6   Shortcomings of Nix

Despite being a powerful tool offering a good user experience, Nix comes with disadvantages. Contradicting the simplicity of the Nix language, Nix as a tool has a steep learning curve. Nix suffers from not being supported on Microsoft's Windows Operating System (OS)—that is, to a limited degree, Nix can compile for Windows, but not on Windows. While there are efforts to port Nix to Windows, it remains unclear whether these will eventually yield a usable implementation.

Also, coming back at the steep learning curve mentioned before, packaging huge applications can become increasingly difficult. While all tools touched in this thesis were reasonably simple to package, this is by no means the norm when looking at monolithic development toolchains grown over decades, such as Xilinx' Vivado. For example, while we successfully packaged Cameo System Modeler and SYSGO's Codeo (including PikeOS), both required a significant portion of reverse engineering, guess work, and Linux knowledge in the process.

5.1.7   Fulfilling More DO-178 Objectives

While we referred to DO-178C constantly throughout this text, we did not analyze in detail how each and every objective from DO-178C can be achieved. For example, we did not provide a strategy to formulate low-level requirements. Another example could be the missing discrimination between normal range and robustness testing by our press-mold approach. Likely, there many more details which require closer inspection if compliance with DO-178C is intended.

5.2   Conclusion

DevOps and Agile are two methodologies which address the lack of flexibility and feedback found in traditional development life cycle models [1, 2]. While there is friction when adapting them for embedded systems [3], both DevOps and Agile are claimed to be suitable for airborne software engineering [4, 5]. Indeed, there is evidence indicating that DevOps' strive for continuous, automated feedback provides real value in avionic developments [4, 6].

In this text, we outline our vision towards adapting DevOps for avionics. The feedback cycle in DevOps, depicted in Fig. 1.2, identifies various activities which are to be connected. To enable DevOps' full potential, all remaining gaps in this cycle need to be filled. We foresee the use of the following tools and methodologies in order to close these gaps:

Rust is a new systems programming language which enables the implementation of high-performance yet safe code without giving up on control [7, 8]. With Rust, we intend to enhance the speed of development, as it emphasizes correct-by-design implementations while discouraging many unsound code constructs. In continuation of our previous publication [9], we further propose Behavior-Driven Development (BDD) as a methodology to maintain a close relationship between requirements and development. Both BDD and Test-Driven Development (TDD) are well suited to complement DevOps and Agile [10, 11]. In addition, BDD satisfies many objectives mandated by DO-178C [12], which is essential for most airborne software engineering. To cope with the increasingly complex process of building avionic software and managing development environments, the Nix package manager is exploited [13]. It allows for reproducible, pure builds of the software at hand, without requiring much work for setting up development environments [14]. Nix flakes, a recent innovation in the Nix ecosystem, further streamline the use of development tools [15]. Last but not least, the stream-based real-time capable monitor RTLola is considered [16]. The full picture of the proposed usage for these tools and techniques in DevOps can be found in Fig. 3.1.

In safety-critical systems, often embedded virtualization is used to segregate multiple applications into separate fault domains [17]. In the aviation industry, this is required too [12, 18]; however, in the context of Integrated Modular Avionics (IMA), it is called partitioning. Now to evaluate our proposal, we integrate the Terrain Awareness and Warning System (TAWS) demonstrator application openTAWS in a partitioned environment—fentISS' XNG. As the development takes place on the GitHub platform, we also try its native Continuous Integration (CI) solution GitHub Actions. In the process, we present a solution to execute the BDD tool Cucumber in a partition to verify requirements on other partitions. As XNG is programmed in and for the C programming language, we also develop a wrapper library, allowing our Rust code to interface XNG's Application Programming Interface (API). Executing our XNG setup on a target computer is elaborate for CI; thus, we use fentISS' SKE to run it.

Overall, our results are encouraging. We find Rust to be of great value in assisting our software design, preventing us from committing many errors. The BDD-based acceptance testing of requirements is not only useful but furthermore allows to easily satisfy many of DO-178C's traceability objectives. Our approach towards testing from a partition is promising to test not only one system but many. Both GitHub Actions and Nix are fine tools for CI. The former shines especially for its supreme integration in the actual development process, offering seamless feedback accessible directly from the code which the feedback refers to. However, it also presents weakness regarding the sharing of build artifacts. Here Nix shines, for offering reusable, reproducible builds. Furthermore, it enables the declarative setup of development environments; with Nix, most tools and builds are only a single command away.

References

1. K. Beck et al., *Manifesto for Agile Software Development* (2001). https://agilemanifesto.org/ (visited on 07/06/2021)
2. J. Davis, R. Daniels, *Effective DevOps—Building a Culture of Collaboration, Affinity and Tooling at Scale* (O'Reilly Media, Sebastopol, 2016). ISBN: 978-1-491-92642-0
3. L.E. Lwakatare, T. Karvonen, T. Sauvola, P. Kuvaja, H.H. Olsson, J. Bosch, M. Oivo, Towards DevOps in the embedded systems domain: why is it so hard? in *2016 49th Hawaii International Conference on System Sciences (HICSS)* (2016), pp. 5437–5446. https://doi.org/10.1109/HICSS.2016.671
4. J. Marsden, A. Windisch, R. Mayo, J. Grossi, J. Villermin, L. Fabre, C. Aventini, ED-12C/DO-178C vs. agile manifesto—a solution to agile development of certifiable avionics systems, in *ERTS 2018* (2018)
5. N. Chaillan. https://www.aftc.af.mil/News/Article-Display/Article/2171467/software-innovati ons-makes-f-16-more-capable/. (visited on 07/12/2021)
6. Air Force Life Cycle Management Center (2020). https://www.aftc.af.mil/News/Article-Display/Article/2171467/software-innovations-makes-f-16-more-capable/ (visited on 07/12/2021)
7. R. Jung, J.-H. Jourdan, R. Krebbers, D. Dreyer, Safe systems programming in rust: the promise and the challenge. Commun. ACM **64**(4), 144–152 (2020). https://doi.org/10.1145/3458337
8. A. Balasubramanian, M.S. Baranowski, A. Burtsev A. Panda, Z. Rakamarić, L. Ryzhyk, System programming in rust: beyond safety, in *Proceedings of the 16th Workshop on Hot Topics in Operating Systems*. HotOS '17 (Association for Computing Machinery, Whistler, 2017), pp. 156–161. ISBN: 9781450350686. https://doi.org/10.1145/3102980.3103006
9. W. Zaeske, U. Durak, C. Torens, Behavior driven development for airborne software engineering. in *AIAA Scitech 2021 Forum* (American Institute of Aeronautics and Astronautics, 2021). https://doi.org/10.2514/6.2021-1917
10. K. Beck, *Test-Driven Development—By Example* (Addison-Wesley Professional, Boston, 2003). ISBN: 978-0-321-14653-3
11. J.F. Smart, *BDD in Action Behavior-Driven Development for the Whole Software Lifecycle* (Manning Publications, Birmingham, 2014). ISBN: 978-1-617-29165-4
12. RTCA, *DO-178C Software Considerations in Airborne Systems and Equipment Certification*. Standard (RTCA, 2011)
13. E. Dolstra, M. de Jonge, E. Visser, Nix: a safe and policy-free system for software deployment, in *LISA '04: Eighteenth Systems Administration Conference* (2004), pp. 79–92

14. E. Dolstra, The Purely Functional Software Deployment Model. Dissertation. Universiteit Utrecht, 2006
15. NixOS Contributors. https://nixos.org/manual/nix/unstable/command-ref/new-cli/nix3-flake.html (visited on 07/19/2021)
16. P. Faymonville, B. Finkbeiner, M. Schledjewski, M. Schwenger, M. Stenger, L. Tentrup, H. Torfah, StreamLAB: stream-based monitoring of cyber physical systems, in *Computer Aided Verification*, ed. by I. Dillig, S. Tasiran (Springer International Publishing, Cham, 2019), pp. 421–431. ISBN: 978-3-030-25540-4
17. G. Heiser, The role of virtualization in embedded systems, in *Proceedings of the 1st Workshop on Isolation and Integration in Embedded Systems*. IIES '08 (Association for Computing Machinery, Glasgow, Scotland, 2008), pp. 11–16. ISBN: 9781605581262. https://doi.org/10.1145/1435458.1435461
18. VxWorks. https://content.cdntwrk.com/files/aT0xMTc0MDM4JnY9MiZpc3N1ZU5hbWU9dnh3b3Jrcy02NTMtbXVsdGktY29yZS1lZGl0aW9uLXByb2R1Y3Qtb3ZlcnZpZXcmY21kPWQmc2lnPTFiMmNkYzI4OGQ5MzczOGQ1MmIzZDA1MDVmNDdlYWEy (visited on 07/13/2021)

Printed in the United States
by Baker & Taylor Publisher Services